ANCHAL SEDA is a prolific social media content creator, presenter and culture champion based in London. With almost a decade spent in the beauty influencer industry, Anchal has singlehandedly built a unique and heart-warming brand that embodies everything it means to be a strong, ambitious, independent woman.

Anchal graduated from the University of Salford with a BA (Hons) in Special Effects and Media Makeup Artistry and moved on to creating inspiring and educational beauty content for makeup lovers around the world. Her platform has allowed her to work with the world's most popular and reputable brands, such as MAC, L'Oréal, Estee Lauder, NARS, Maybelline, the BBC, and many more.

Following on from her popular 'Brown Girl Confessions' YouTube series, Anchal launched her podcast *What Would The Aunties Say?* to address taboo topics within South Asian culture that had personally impacted her life and were very close to her heart. It was featured in Spotify's 'best podcast of the week' playlist and rated 5 stars on Apple Music. Every step and misstep along Anchal's incredible journey has led her to begin an exciting new chapter as the author of her debut book, which shares the same title as her successful podcast.

WHAT WOULD THE AUNTIES SAY?

A brown girl's guide to being yourself
and living your best life

ANCHAL SEDA

GALLERY BOOKS UK

First published in Great Britain by Gallery Books UK, an imprint of
Simon & Schuster UK Ltd, 2021

1 3 5 7 9 10 8 6 4 2

Simon & Schuster UK Ltd
1st Floor
222 Gray's Inn Road
London WC1X 8HB

www.simonandschuster.co.uk
www.simonandschuster.com.au
www.simonandschuster.co.in

Simon & Schuster Australia, Sydney
Simon & Schuster India, New Delhi

A CIP catalogue record for this book is available from the British Library

Hardback ISBN: 978-1-3985-0560-5
Trade Paperback ISBN: 978-1-3985-0561-2
eBook ISBN: 978-1-3985-0562-9

Typeset in Palatino by M Rules
Printed in the UK by CPI Group (UK) Ltd, Croydon, CR0 4YY

For my three beautiful nieces:
Diya, Riva & Saachi.

The future brown girls. I hope to be the Auntie you can forever turn to, to share your wildest moments with and not feel judged or scared. I promise to laugh with you, cry with you, gossip with you about boys, and help you pick outfits for your nights out, but more importantly, I promise to protect you. I've got your back. I want you to know that you are loved, you are worthy, and you are more than capable to do anything you want to in life.

I love you more than words could ever describe.

Your Anchal Masi

CONTENTS

I

'IS THIS THE LITTLE GIRL I REMEMBER?'

Makeup artist turned author? Not something you see every day, I know. So, how did that happen, you ask?

Well, let me talk you through it.

My name is Anchal, and I'm a British Indian girl, born and raised in London. (I'm Punjabi, to be specific – and believe me, Indian people always want to know the specifics!)

I come from a pretty large family. I'm the youngest of three girls, and I also have a younger brother. My extended family is absolutely enormous, so I won't bother trying to list them all out. For a start, I don't think I could even count how many cousins I have. This is quite typical – it's considered a little strange if you're Indian and your family is small!

Growing up, it was all too easy to compare myself to my siblings. It could sometimes be very difficult, to tell you the truth. I wasn't the most academic student, which meant the path before me couldn't be defined by grades and exams.

I was always a much more creative person, wanting to spend my time doing practical things. I loved tasks where I could create something and see a finished product. I remember being very young when the first ever webcams came out, and my dad bought us one. I would record and host my own shows – and casually force my brother to be a guest so I could interview someone.

At ten years old, I asked for a karaoke machine for my birthday. It was the most amazing karaoke ever: it had a CD *and* a tape player! I'd play multiple characters on the microphone and get into serious debates with myself. I'd record R&B songs on the cassettes and throw in music intervals – true radio presenter style! There I was, with my very own one-girl radio show.

In most Indian families, the idea of pursuing something creative or artistic isn't generally encouraged or explored; in fact, it's simply not understood. So, that creative route didn't feel like a realistic career option for me. Even considering it as a possibility seemed like a waste of time.

So, I tried to do what was expected of me. I tried to follow the 'respected' and 'right' path. I essentially forced myself through education, trying to mould myself into a person I'm not.

But trying to be someone else never works for long, and one day, I just gave up. It was a relief not to have to pretend any more. At the same time, though, I had no plans of where to go next.

I really struggled to figure out what I wanted to do with my life, constantly asking myself, *What are you good at?*

My family would always tell me the same thing: that I'm

caring. It's true – I do care about my friends and family, so much. So, I decided to start a nursing course. That's a caring profession, not to mention one that's respected in the Indian community, so it had to be the path for me, right?

Unfortunately, I had no interest in it whatsoever. It's a wonderful profession, but it's not who I am. I went into it because it seemed like the right thing on paper, not because it was right for me.

Then, one day, it happened. I was on a hospital placement and I quite literally had an epiphany.

Throughout the whole course that year, doing the placement was the best part for me (obviously, because it was practical). I remember they had put me on a men's gastro ward – the least glamorous setting you could imagine. One old man couldn't feed himself breakfast, so I offered to help. I sat there, feeding him his porridge, asking him about his tattoos, and he shared all his life stories with me.

But my mind couldn't help but wander. I stopped, and I looked around. I realised that, although this was something I could do for now, I couldn't see myself as a nurse for the next twenty, thirty, forty years.

I know how very silly and shallow it might sound, but I missed having my nails done. I missed putting makeup on. I missed the things that made me feel like me.

I thought about my mum and how she's so elegant (she really is #goals for me). I want to be like her when I'm older – beautiful, stylish and happy with who she is.

As I sat there listening to this very nice old man talk about his life, I wondered what I would say when looking back on my own life one day. Would I be proud, happy, satisfied – or full of regrets for not having pursued a career I was genuinely enthusiastic about?

And it just came to me.

I decided, right then and there, that I wanted to become a makeup artist. It was what I genuinely loved doing. It involved people, which was important to me, but also let me exhibit my creative flair. Finally, I'd found something that wholly suited me.

I talked to my parents. They definitely weren't expecting it (to be honest, none of us ever knew what to expect from me). I did my best to explain why it would be the perfect step for me, in the hope they'd understand.

Either way, I didn't give them much time to think about it. Me being me, I just knew I *had* to do it – I had to get my way. So I enrolled myself onto some courses and simply got on with it.

I left my nursing course and attended the University of Salford in Manchester to study a foundation degree in Special Effects and Media Makeup Artistry, then went on to do a bachelor's degree in the same subject. It was like nothing I'd ever experienced before – for the first time in my life, I was learning something I genuinely cared about, and it made a serious difference to both my achievement and enjoyment levels.

During my time at university, I naturally found myself watching a lot of makeup videos and tutorials on YouTube. I very quickly noticed that there wasn't really anyone like me – particularly anyone who shared my skin colour or cultural background – doing this sort of stuff. There were also rarely people who switched to makeup a bit later in life. Many of them had gone into the profession straight from school, and talked as though that was a given. Of all the amazing makeup artists I discovered, I couldn't see any I was able to relate to – at least not any that had expert knowledge in makeup.

Why not do it myself, I thought? So, in 2013 – my second year of university – I decided to start my own YouTube channel.

After uploading two videos on YouTube, and receiving about forty views total (from my most dedicated fans of all – my friends and family), I decided to enter a huge beauty competition on a channel called Daily Mix. I knew it was a gigantic step, and probably wishful thinking. The competition was run by the biggest makeup YouTubers at the time, Sam and Nic from Pixiwoo. It was the first time I'd ever vlogged. I figured my tiny YouTube presence would barely register on their radar, and I was just grateful for the experience.

I ended up winning.

I couldn't believe it. I'd never won anything in my life before – certainly nothing that was this important to me.

I don't know why they picked me, why I stood out. My videos were simple makeup tutorials, and I'd never vlogged before the competition. I was up against people who had been creating YouTube content for much longer, who had built a following and were used to being in front of the camera. I remember feeling like a small fish in a big pond full of people who were super confident and almost a little *too* sure of themselves. They knew they were worth a win, and that's what they wanted.

If I'm honest, though, winning wasn't what mattered. I was there because I wanted to be part of something I enjoyed. That's it.

The competition only motivated me to take my YouTube channel more seriously, and since then I've continued to upload makeup videos regularly, about twice a week.

I finished university, and soon had a full-time job working on a makeup counter for MAC, before moving on to a customer service team at Charlotte Tilbury. It was hectic, especially as I was running my YouTube channel at the same time. The hustle didn't stop for me. I'd work my usual full-time hours, then come home excited to film and edit makeup looks until the early hours. I would repeat this demanding routine daily, all the while trying to maintain the relationship I was in at the time and keep up a social life.

Eventually I gave up the 'day job' so I could pursue my career on social media. I knew I was burning myself at both ends, and it was the right time.

During this period, however, I found that I was searching for something deeper and more meaningful beyond creating simple makeup tutorials – something that made me feel more fulfilled.

As I reached my mid-twenties, my childhood issues and family dynamics started resurfacing. You see, when I was much younger, we went through quite a lot as a family. My dad was, in a weird way, both present and absent at the same time. He was there physically, but it didn't feel like he was there emotionally.

He was more of a traditional Indian dad: there to support you financially, but not particularly in any other way.

I suppose that was his way of showing his presence and support – his love. Of course, we were grateful, but it was never truly enough. As much as buying us the best and latest things was all very well and good, we quickly got to a point where we'd rather go without those shiny new things if it meant we could have quality time with him. We yearned for him to be interested in what we were doing with our lives, to actually get to know us as people and individuals. Instead, he seemed to always view us as little children. He could buy us things to keep us quiet, and for anything more complicated, we could go to our mum. I certainly couldn't approach him about a boy I liked in school, or have conversations about general passions and dreams. It was very much a 'needs must' type of relationship.

I believe he was the same way with us kids as he was with our mum, and our mum's way of coping was to turn to spirituality and religion. For the rest of us, especially as children, the best advice to follow was very much, 'Keep your head down and get on with it.' It got very tough for a while – but the whole situation brought us so much closer as siblings, and to our mum, because we all went through it together. Eventually, things started to settle down, and we were asked to forgive and forget. We were all tired of the ongoing drama – myself, my siblings and my mum. We were tired of the disagreements, disputes and tears, of asking for more and not receiving much back.

So we did exactly as we were asked.

It was only many years later that I realised just how hard it can be to truly forgive, and truly forget. As I grew older, I started to notice some of my dad's behaviours that I didn't particularly agree with. I hadn't noticed them when I was younger, but now I was becoming more my own person, it gradually became apparent to me how much we clashed, and how we had such massive differences of opinions on some matters. In a lot of ways, our personalities are very similar: we're two very bold and strong characters, but with two completely opposite views on most things – a recipe for conflict. It was difficult to adjust, as an adult – it almost felt as if he was now somewhat emotionally present in our lives, where he hadn't been for so long. But I was no longer a child that had to do as I was told; I was now a young woman, one who had formed her own thoughts, ideas and opinions. At this stage, I felt resentment for not being able to get closure on our family situation, and for never receiving an apology for everything we'd been put through.

Most of all, I realised I was censoring how I spoke on my YouTube channel. I was holding back on certain subjects because I was too afraid to say something my dad, his family and our culture would disagree with. It was a shame, because my YouTube channel had become such an important mental outlet for me.

Over the years, I never felt I could openly speak about my own struggles or emotions with the people around me. They just wouldn't get it; they wouldn't be able to relate. Rather than trying to navigate that minefield, I decided instead to create videos offering advice to other Indian, Bangladeshi and Pakistani girls like me. This was my way of inspiring South Asian girls to do and feel better, while indirectly enabling me to say things to my dad that I couldn't in person.

He watches my videos religiously, you see. He really has been my number-one fan ever since the very start (well, maybe ever since I won the competition, and he could finally see the potential for success in what I was doing). I can literally hear my voice echo through the house all day, because he watches each of my videos the second I post them – as if I'm not sick enough of listening to my own voice from the hours of editing!

This meant I was able to communicate my thoughts and feelings to my dad, filtered through the face of my channel, which was very freeing in so many ways. But it wasn't the same as being fully, directly open. I still lived in fear of my dad's disapproval, and my mum's worry. Even worse, I was constantly aware of the different ways my huge Indian family and community could – and would – interfere. If they saw something they didn't like, anything at all, then the next time they spoke to my parents: what would the Aunties say?

If I spoke the 'wrong' words, or posted a picture of myself in a bikini at a pool party (because where else would I wear it?), the Aunties wouldn't take long to pick up the phone and ask if my parents had seen it, or if I should be doing and saying such things. Every single thing I did was under scrutiny, all the time.

I didn't want to keep hiding my real thoughts and opinions, my real personality, any more. I've always been talkative, I've always been opinionated, and a lot of the time I'm very direct with people. (I'm not sure if that last point is a good or a bad thing, but hey – that's me!) How could I be online discussing 'Brown Girl Problems', but limiting the advice I offered others to what I felt was suitable for my dad or extended family to hear? That wasn't fair on all the girls who followed me on social media whom I'd built up a connection with over the years, who were strong and brave enough to share their stories.

Those fearless girls inspired me. I had to have courage, just like them. And so, I took the decision to start therapy, and get some support with the things I was struggling to adjust to. It wasn't the easiest step to take – mental health awareness is currently pretty lacking in South Asian communities, and the idea of seeing a therapist isn't understood at all (more on this later). But it was brilliant; one of the best decisions I've ever made. It gave me the confidence to make the switch from speaking indirectly to my dad in my videos to speaking openly on everything, anything and, well, everyone!

It also helped me, slowly, to release the guilt I'd built up for having my own opinions and expressing them to my dad. In some ways, it's helped our relationship. Of course, we still don't agree on most things, but at least we can both unapologetically be ourselves.

The most incredible thing was, the minute I dropped the fear and stopped caring, so did the Aunties. I think we overthink things sometimes. Personally, I discovered that the more I showed my fear of what people said and thought of me, the more I would see and hear it. But the minute it became something that wasn't important, I noticed quickly how little other people actually care.

My videos proved popular, which meant I increasingly found that I was creating a space for the *real* voice of brown girls around the world – somewhere we could all be heard, all sharing similar struggles and situations. This led me to start my podcast, where I speak honestly on all sorts of topics, and share other brown girl problems, intimate feelings and experiences.

And this has now brought me here, to you, writing this book! In it, I'll talk about our problems as brown girls – but also the amazing experiences we're lucky to be a part of, as well as giving you a bunch of insights and wisdom to help each other out.

Consider this the ultimate guide to being a brown girl: how to be yourself, live your life, and, of course, deal with the Aunties.

2

'WHY CAN'T YOU BE MORE LIKE HER?'

Who are the brown girls?

Typically, 'brown girls' is a slang term, but it's one that is pretty much instantly recognised by the community. It's important to remember that it's an inclusive, umbrella term, and it welcomes all girls from South Asia.

We come from a wide variety of backgrounds and religions. Each of us is so diverse and distinctive, it's impossible to list all the ways. Our shared culture remains strong, however, and ties us together with similar life experiences, struggles and understandings of being a brown girl. Despite the numerous things I may not have in common with another brown girl, we'll still *get* each other on a fundamental level.

We come in an array of different, beautiful skin tones, and we speak a number of melodic languages in various dialects.

We come from:

- India
- Pakistan
- Bangladesh
- Nepal
- Sri Lanka
- Afghanistan
- Bhutan
- the Maldives

And people from plenty of other places, all over the world, may identify as *desi* – in other words, of the Indian subcontinent and worldwide diaspora.

The diaspora is a key part of understanding who we brown girls are. Our roots are strong and stable, and tied into a specific geographic area – but we live and thrive all over the globe. We're travellers. We're adventurers. We're not tied down to any one place.

That means we're not bound to any one culture, either. I speak as one of more than three million British Asians. We brown girls have taken the traditions of thousands of years, and brought them to renewed life in the West. Britain has the South Asian community to thank for the incredible local curry houses, and for throwing the most magnificently extravagant weddings the country has ever seen.

Naturally, it's not just one-way; the West has influenced us, too.

We brown girls are the embodiment of something spectacular. We live and breathe the fusion of East and West. All of us exist on a worldwide spectrum, meaning there are an infinite number of different ways to balance influences from all around the world and still be a proud, valid brown girl.

I'm not a fan of categorising and grouping people; every individual person is unique, and no one can ever wholly fit the confines of a label. But speaking in broad terms can help those who aren't familiar to get a better idea of the typical types of brown girl you'll encounter in the West. And it can help to explain why we're so different, yet so similar.

Most brown girls will fall into these categories in some way, and many may be a combination of a few. Some might change depending on where they are, or what they're doing – or whether an Auntie is around.

Nevertheless, you're sure to have met the following brown girls. You may even recognise yourself ...

Wild West: The Western brown girl

The Wild West brown girl probably has parents that moved to a Western country when they were young, or were even born there themselves. As a result, the Wild West brown girl was able to absorb Western culture from a young age.

This tends to mean there's a certain level of casualness about her. She's a little more relaxed, and a little less rigid. The Wild West brown girl might find it easier to speak to her parents openly about what's on her mind, and often experiences significantly less pressure to stick to traditional cultural values. She probably doesn't speak any family languages, so all her conversations are in English.

Don't be fooled into thinking the Wild West brown girl is ashamed of her roots – she isn't. Like most brown girls, she loves her family and respects her culture. But she absolutely doesn't devote her time or energy to upholding the traditions, most of which are completely irrelevant to her.

Even so, the Wild West brown girl isn't immune to Auntie's judgement. In fact, it's highly likely that she's the most frequent victim of the Aunties' gossiping, because she strays so far from their very particular standards.

The Wild West brown girl is into her Hollywood movies: anything from sci-fi, to horror, to drama, to a good old chick flick. This babe *loves* music – she's able to get down to pretty much anything. But you probably won't hear her playing Bollywood or Bhangra music out of her car.

At a wedding, you'll find her at the bar or on the dance floor. She's there for a good time, not a long time. She'll probably end up skipping dinner, because she's not got time for food when the DJ is that good!

On-the-Fence: The Western/Native brown girl

The On-the-Fence brown girl usually has parents who moved to a Western country much later in life. Perhaps she herself moved to a Western country while still quite young, but spent her formative years in South Asia.

Because of the mix of influences she's grown up with, this brown girl is adaptable and versatile. She'll happily mix with all types of cultures, while still acknowledging her roots and being proud of them. She has some freedom, and probably isn't dictated to too much about her career or clothing choices. But she doesn't get to go all out, either. Speaking to her parents about her love life **won't** happen; she may have to do some lying and sneaking around to get away with what she wants.

The Aunties like to watch out for this one. They're not convinced by all her apparent virtues – despite her best efforts, they suspect she's hiding something. They keep an extra watchful eye on this brown girl, hoping to catch her out at some point so they can spill the tea over her exploits.

The On-the-Fence brown girl is mostly into her Hollywood rom-coms and dramas – she'll be at the cinema watching the latest box office hit. But she also enjoys a Bollywood session here and there: she probably has one or two favourites that her mum showed her on a rainy afternoon.

In terms of music, she prefers her hip-hop and R&B, or she'll be dabbling in Western rock and pop. But she loves to get down to Bhangra at a wedding, and the dance floor is exactly where you'll find her. Either that, or she's found a hidden spot tucked away in the corner of the building, where she can whisper-flirt with the handsome guy she's just met.

By-the-Book: The Native brown girl

The By-the-Book brown girl most likely has pretty strict parents. They won't consider themselves strict, of course, but they feel strongly about their children learning traditional ways. This means the By-the-Book brown girl has a very good understanding of her culture. It's highly likely she speaks her family language fluently, and is inclined to wear Indian and other South Asian outfits.

None of this is remotely a bad thing – the By-the-Book brown girl is highly respected for the way she stays true to what she believes in. But sometimes, she can take it a little too far – when she *only* accepts traditional values, there's a risk she'll become too judgemental for other, more Westernised brown girls to feel truly comfortable around.

In general, though, the By-the-Book brown girl tends to be friends with other By-the-Book brown girls. These friendships are strong, and very trust-based; the best way they can have some freedom and go out is by telling their parents they're at each other's houses. It's not unusual for a friendship between two By-the-Book brown girls to effort-lessly last a lifetime.

The Aunties typically like this brown girl a lot – she probably reminds them of themselves. This is the brown girl that the Aunties will be holding up as the ultimate ideal; the one other brown girls are told to be more like. However, one step out of line, and she'll be next in the Aunties' firing line. And she'll probably get it worst of all.

The By-the-Book brown girl loves her classic Bollywood films – anything starring Shah Rukh Khan, and she'll be the first one at the screening! – all the legends like DDLJ (*Dilwale Dulhania Le Jayenge*), K3G (*Kabhi Khushi Kabhie Gham*) and KKHH (*Kuch Kuch Hota Hai*). (Bollywood loves to give its movies long names, then abbreviate them into short letters – don't ask me why!)

Obviously, because of all her extensive cultural knowl-edge, she's a Bollywood and Bhangra queen who knows all the routines – she may even be part of a dance squad. You'll definitely see her showing off her immense skills on the dance floor at a wedding. But she'll most certainly make time to speak to the Aunties and other guests at the tables; she wouldn't want to be impolite and ruin her family's reputation.

That's an overview of who we brown girls are, and the things we may or may not have in common. The majority of brown girls will recognise themselves, at least a little.

So what about me? Which brown girl am I?

Like most brown girls, I can definitely say I'm never just one type. I can go between being By-the-Book to totally Wild West. It can depend on where I am, and what I'm doing. Often things change depending on the context of your life in that time – I'm a very different brown girl at home compared to when I was at uni. And I'm a very different brown girl now, as a confident, experienced woman, than I was as a young teenager.

I guess it's the same for most of us, isn't it? We start off doing what our parents want; that's the way we're raised. So, as children, we automatically accompany everything we do with worrying about what other people, like the Aunties, will say.

As we become adults, though, and get to know ourselves more, we begin to learn what truly makes us feel most content.

Some of us decide to double down and find our very best selves when we put Asian traditions at the core of everything we do. Meanwhile, some of us take a diverging path, and find ourselves in new ways that also embrace Western values.

You might be a brown girl who subscribes to a certain lifestyle, and meet another brown girl who's so completely opposite to you that it's difficult to see anything in common at all.

But what unites us is much stronger than what differentiates us.

We care about our families. We use all the methods at our disposal to avoid the merciless glare of the Aunties. And we throw the best weddings *ever*.

The most important thing to remember as a brown girl is that every single one of us matters. As long as we're not hurting anyone, then the choices each of us make in our own lives should always be respected.

The truth is, no matter what you do, you're always going to be in someone's bad books. Brown girls often do their best to please the people around them, but the fact of the matter is, some people are utterly impossible to please.

So I suggest that we brown girls stop trying to please everyone, and instead focus on ourselves. Whatever kind of brown girl you choose to be, follow the road in life that makes you the happiest.

I know it's not always easy, though. Especially when the Aunties are watching and waiting for your next move.

3

'DON'T YOU REMEMBER YOUR AUNTIE?'

Let's just say that if you were walking down the street with your boyfriend, you'd want to make pretty sure your Auntie didn't catch you holding hands. In fact, you'd probably want be certain that she hasn't seen you within two metres of one another (pandemic or no pandemic).

Practically before you've even had the time to raise your hand to wave hello (or to hide your face in the vain hope she didn't see you), she'll somehow have managed to inform your parents, your siblings, your extended family, every Asian person in the local community, and some random old lady she knows in Mumbai: she saw you *with a boy*.

So who is this woman we all fear so much, this ever-present and seemingly unstoppable presence?

An Auntie is an extended family member; that much we all already knew.

But it doesn't stop there, not in Asian culture. Every single older Asian woman you ever meet – your mum's friend, your friend's mum, the lady in the supermarket that's serving you, the woman that helps you in the bank, or the stranger you walk past on the street who gives you a motherly smile – they're *all* Aunties.

And it's fully encouraged that you address them as such, out loud. It doesn't matter if you've never met them before. No one will frown at you or try to remember whether you're some long-lost niece of theirs; instead, they'll happily bring you in for an Auntie hug and kiss.

However, you have to be careful not to throw around the word too casually, either. Using 'Auntie' for a younger woman, or a soon-to-be-Auntie that somehow isn't quite yet ready to be an Auntie, can easily be taken as an insult – you're basically implying you think they look older than they were hoping they did. Yes, it's all pretty random, and extremely tricky to navigate!

To make matters even more tough, at almost every large family event, such as a wedding, without a doubt at some point you'll have an Auntie come over to you and say, 'Don't you remember me?' And nine times out of ten, no, no you don't remember her. *At all.*

It happens to me at nearly every wedding I go to. I'll be talking to relatives I haven't seen in a while. Or I'll be in the middle of the dance floor. I'll be lost in the crowd somewhere, just minding my own business. But my parents, without fail, will always spot me. They'll excitedly drag me away by the arm, or be waving at me frantically to come over to them. It's even worse when your own parents start with, 'Anchal, say hello to Auntie. Do you remember her?'

All I'm thinking, with a fake grin frozen on my face, is – why, oh why, would you ask me if I remember her *when she's standing right here?*

But it happens, every time. So you smile and nod, and pretend you have a whole collection of fond memories with Auntie. Like that time we had a family BBQ with fifty other guests. Or that time at so-and-so's wedding. As a brown girl, you'll probably get used to having long, reminiscent conversations with random Aunties you swear you've never seen before in your life.

But whether you remember her or not, there are some general rules that apply to all Aunties.

The Aunties are normally known for gossiping and stirring problems within families. Their all-time favourite activity is passing judgement (whether out loud by lecturing you directly, or more subtly, say, through a permanently disapproving look in their eyes). They're often busy trying to find out every last detail about your life, in the apparent hopes of discovering a new scandal to tell everyone about.

Every single Auntie is somehow friends with every single other Auntie who lives nearby. And they love a good old 'kitty party' – their monthly meet-up where they let their hair down, away from their husbands, and really get the chance to share the hottest news. That means, if you were caught holding hands with your boyfriend on the street, you'll probably be the number-one discussion point that month.

Saying that, the Aunties aren't *all* bad. They may love a bit of tea-spilling, but they can also be wise, and caring, and strong.

Aside from an excuse to see their friends, the purpose of the monthly Auntie gatherings is for each member of the kitty to contribute some money. Whoever is hosting that month gets the entire pot to buy whatever they wish. It's a way for the Aunties to socialise, catch up with old friends and make new ones – but they also get themselves a nice financial boost, and that's never a bad thing. In Pakistani culture it's known as 'committee' and is done less for the social aspect and more overtly for the financial benefit – but either way, it's a win-win for the Aunties. They're pretty savvy.

The Aunties are much more affectionate than they may initially seem. They've learned so much from their years on the planet, and they can pass on valuable advice to young brown girls. They often want to help guide you, so you don't make the same mistakes they made. I love those Aunties – the ones that really root for you. There are even those who want to vicariously live through you, and they always do what they can to encourage you to become your best self.

So how to know when to ignore an Auntie's scolding, and when to follow their sage advice?

You have to be careful – not all Aunties are the same. They come in all sorts of shapes and sizes and different levels of heat: mild, spicy and hot. Be very cautious when trying to handle a spice level above your limit.

Mild Auntie

This is the versatile Auntie. She fits in with the young crowd *and* the more mature ladies, being admired and respected by all. She's chatty, friendly, bubbly, and fashionable too – both in Asian and Western styles.

She's very supportive, and you can go to her if you need a bit of help with something. She'll give you some tea and cake, and a shoulder to cry on if you need it. The Mild

Auntie will be the one who's a little understanding about you having a boyfriend, and won't immediately condemn you for it. However, you don't want to tell her *too* much, as she still can't help loving a bit of a local scandal.

She's a Bollywood queen and can rock the film routines, but she enjoys Hollywood too, and will catch the latest block-busters. At a wedding she'll be at the bar, allowing herself a couple of drinks before she lets loose on the dance floor. She can also bob her head to a little hip-hop and chart music.

Spicy Auntie

This Auntie is gentle, kind and very loving. She's abundantly generous, and wants to feed you your favourite meal whenever you go over to her house. Even if you're not hungry, she insists on keeping you fed, or she won't feel she's done her duty. And then she'll give you leftovers in a Tupperware box to take home. Your health and happiness matter a lot to her.

But watch out! She has a solid, sprawling group of friends and relatives she'll happily tell your business to in her many WhatsApp group chats. She's the type to judge you before she truly understands your situation. And by the time she understands – she's already told everyone! What's frustrating is that she disguises her tendencies with her spiritual and religious ways. People might think she's a little angel, always praying to God, but she'll have no shame spilling your tea in the temple.

She loves listening to *shabad* (religious music) and hymns, but of course she's another Bollywood-loving queen, who'll fit in her Indian films between religious programmes and documentaries about South Asian history. At a wedding she'll stick to chatting with friends at the table.

Hot Auntie

Uh oh – this Auntie is the worst of the worst. Say the absolute minimum to her; you'll learn this the hard way if you become a victim of her loose mouth. She has no shame in telling everyone your business, and she'll twist it to put her own critical spin on it. She'll drag it on for as long as she can, presumably because she really doesn't have anything exciting going on in her life.

What's worse, she usually has some drama cooking in her own family. Don't bother pointing it out, though – she'll quite happily gloss over it and throw her two pence where it isn't needed elsewhere. She's not afraid to make snide comments and pick on your image – she'll do it in front of a room full of people, as well.

Despite all this, somehow this Auntie is always 'popular' among family members. She definitely has her fair share of wisdom, and loyalty – it'd just be helpful if she could tone down the constant fault-finding.

She only watches Bollywood, and she only listens to Bollywood. She has no interest in broadening her cultural knowledge beyond what she knows – and anyway, her Indian family dramas are exactly where she learned to play the wicked witch.

At a wedding, she is *everywhere*. She'll be at the table chatting with the Aunties one minute, the next she's on the dance floor, and then you'll catch her having a gossip in the bathroom. The one place you absolutely will *not* catch her is at the bar – she despises the mere idea of alcohol. She won't even be seen collecting drinks for someone else; she has an image to protect, after all.

As you can see, there is a spectrum of different Aunties. Just like the brown girls, most Aunties will not neatly fit into a single stereotype; they can often flit between them, or be combinations.

It's clear they all love a gossip. Yes, for some, it's with malicious intent – but others just want to be in the loop of what's going on in the family. Even the most loving, careful and respectful of Aunties won't be afraid to pick up the phone and share the latest news.

I have a *Masi*, which is the word for 'mother's sister' in Punjabi. She's also known as a second mum and, most of the time, the best Auntie you'll have, in the most nurturing and positive way. But even my *Masi*, who has the biggest heart, who's so generous and is a dedicated woman of God, will always be able to spill some tea.

I mean, we all love a bit of gossip, don't we?

The Aunties and us, we're not so different. A brown girl fears that the Aunties' comments will ruin her reputation and reveal her secrets. It's my belief that the Aunties have gone through the same fears themselves. A big part of their judgemental streak is actually, in a way, them projecting and passing on their own deep insecurities.

When an Auntie chides you about getting married by a certain age, it might be that they themselves got married later than they wanted to, or never married. When they analyse how fair or dark your skin colour is (a property which allegedly determines your suitability for marriage), it might be because they've experienced comments about their own complexion when younger. When they throw in pressure and criticism around exactly which boy you end up marrying, you can guarantee they went through the same thing at your age – probably ten times as bad.

It's not fair for the Aunties to take their own poor experiences and direct them at us. Of course they should be more sensitive to what we young brown girls need, and try to build us up instead of knocking us down. But, even when they're at their most conniving and manipulative, the Aunties are still human. They still feel genuine warmth, and they still enjoy a good laugh, and getting lost in a long, engrossing film. They're fierce about protecting the people they love from embarrassment and disappointment.

It's just that, sometimes, they can be a little *too* fierce.

Although I speak of the Aunties and categorise them as though they're separate from me, I'm actually an Auntie myself. I have three beautiful nieces who call me *Masi*. And I have to laugh sometimes, because when I'm with my sisters and we sit over a cup of tea and talk about the latest family shenanigans, I notice that we're becoming *those* Aunties.

As long as I stay pretty mild, I'm completely okay with that. I'm the cool Auntie for sure.

4

'GIRLS THESE DAYS ARE GETTING TOO MODERN'

Oh no! Too *modern?* The absolute worst thing a girl could be!

By 'modern', they really mean 'Westernised'.

If you're a Wild West brown girl, you can expect to hear the word 'modern' thrown at you a lot.

On-the-Fence? Same.

By-the-Book? Same. No, really. You might not hear it as much as the other brown girls, but you'll hear it. It doesn't matter how much you adhere to Indian traditions; you *will* be told that some seemingly innocent thing you've done is just too 'modern'.

Imagine you're a foodie, and you love to take photos of the amazing meals you eat. You've just posted a photo on Instagram of an incredible gourmet burger you've ordered at a new restaurant.

Your typical Mild Auntie will be a bit disappointed. Sure, the burger looks nice and all. But you *always* post photos of burgers, or pizza, or fish and chips. Just once, couldn't you post a photo of a nice Asian meal? What about the lovely curry she made you last weekend? Didn't that deserve to go on Instagram? No. You always seem to go for the *modern* cuisine.

Your typical Spicy Auntie will be even less thrilled. Why does all of this have to go on Instagram at all? What's the point of plastering everything on the internet for others to see? She prefers the good old days when you spoke to people in person, and 'posting a photo' meant in an envelope, not online. She has no time for these *modern* pursuits. (Unless it's her own Instagram, of course, and she wants to show everyone back home all the *modern* things she gets up to. Like visits to the casino, or even a girls' holiday. Again, double standards much, Auntie?)

Obviously, the Hot Auntie will agree with all of this condemnation. In addition, her eagle eye will somehow catch the tiny patch in the bottom corner of the photo, where your knee is showing. Your *bare* knee! She'll wonder how on earth you could go out wearing a skirt that falls to mid-thigh – so scandalous! Although, if you were wearing ripped jeans, she probably wouldn't be happy either. Anything that isn't a full-on sari or salwar kameez is definitely, definitely too *modern*.

It's funny. If a brown girl embraces a part of Western culture, no matter how small or inconsequential, then the Aunties seem to treat it as some kind of failure. It's almost as if it's shameful to be a brown girl that speaks up, a brown girl that has independence or a brown girl that proudly makes her own decisions.

Does this come from a place of jealousy, because girls these days are able to do things that the Aunties weren't? Is it that the Aunties couldn't eat burgers or wear jeans when they were young, and they envy us because we can?

Or is it more about the Aunties wanting to keep their girls traditional? Is it that their devotion to Asian traditions is so strong that anyone who strays away is immediately some kind of traitor?

Maybe it's controversial but, actually, I believe it's jealousy.

Think about it. None of the Aunties in our local communities are fully, 100 per cent devoted to Asian traditions over Western ones. I can say that with confidence. Why? Because they live in the West. They moved, whether with their families or off their own back, away from the Asian countries of their ancestors. Yes, they respect and adore their traditional cultures, but they're still a little Westernised, even if it's by default. If they genuinely believed that a brown girl being too 'modern' betrays their roots, then the Aunties would be traitors just as much as any of us.

Instead, I truly believe it's about jealousy, and resentment. We brown girls these days are so lucky – we get to explore and embrace parts of both cultures. The Aunties never had that choice.

No wonder they're so strict with us, right? Can we blame them?

Well, yes, we can. Sometimes.

First of all, one thing I'd like to point out to the Aunties is that girls these days don't *actually* get to do the things that the Aunties didn't. It's not like our generation suddenly had all the rules removed, and were given complete freedom. It's just that we're not daunted by the need to sneak around.

And hey, let's be serious here – we can't honestly pretend that all Aunties have been saints for their entire lives. Most of them will never admit it, but we know that they too were young brown girls at one point, and they too had to sneak around to see their secret love interests. That's why all the many, many Bollywood movies about forbidden love affairs have been so popular for so many decades – they're practically documentaries for the Aunties.

I do wonder whether a lot of the anti-Western attitudes are tied into that very profound and important thing: love, and who you give your heart to versus who you wind up spending your life with. Is it those Aunties who had to have arranged marriages, who had to follow rules that dictated their deepest emotions, who are now the most judgemental ones? Does seeing young brown girls living freely rub them up the wrong way, because they could never give their own feelings free rein?

And do they call it all 'modern' because that's easier than admitting they're jealous?

The 'modern' accusation reveals a lot about the way the brown community has found homes all over the world. When you're away from the place of your family's oldest traditions, anything different will naturally seem new, unprecedented, *modern*. It's an insight into how the diaspora can give a sense of homelessness. Sure, the land you've settled in has its own established traditions and cultures, but to you they are completely brand new.

For the parents and grandparents that emigrated to a

Western country later in their lives, I can only imagine how difficult it must have been to adapt in a completely new environment. New smells, new sounds, and for some even a whole new language. Harsh voices mispronouncing their names time and time again. A sea of faces that all look the same, and yet constantly completely unfamiliar.

Our grandparents and parents were able to do all of this. They uprooted their entire lives, with only a faint hope of better things. They came to entirely foreign lands and started over from scratch. They bore the stares, the giggles and the loneliness. They kept going, and kept going, and kept going. How many of us now can honestly say we would be able to do the same?

I admire their bravery; I know that I would definitely struggle to move to a place where I knew absolutely no one, and had to start a new life. I'm so used to the life I know that being wrenched out of it would be insanely difficult.

I agree we mustn't lose our roots and where we come from – they are a vital, and beautiful, part of the brown girl experience. However, we also have to become accustomed to Western standards and practices. It would be hypocritical to build a life in a country, take advantage of its benefits and opportunities, and yet condemn every single thing it stands for.

Sometimes I'm really not sure what our families expected when they emigrated to a Western country. Did they think they'd be able to raise their children without an ounce of influence from the place they're actually living?

Many of us brown girls were born and raised in Western countries, while others have had to move at a young age and adapt. I have lived in London all my life, meaning I've been lucky enough to be around all sorts of different ethnicities, backgrounds, cultures and languages.

At home, my parents spoke Punjabi to us as babies, as they knew we would go to school and learn English there. It wasn't because they couldn't speak English themselves; in fact they speak it incredibly well, with only a little accent betraying that they're not native English speakers.

I'm grateful to have been immersed in both languages. As you're growing up, it's great to know you can take part in the conversations that go on at home, or even overhear when the Aunties are snitching and gossiping, because we all know the tea is always hotter when they can say it in their mother tongue. That's when they really let loose. If you don't speak the language, it's probably a good thing as you do *not* want to know what those two cackling old Indian ladies on the bus are saying about you.

Being bilingual, even just a little, is great for so many reasons – but it can create difficulties, too. Maybe you're at school, or work, and you're involving yourself in a fascinating conversation. All of a sudden you start to stutter on your words, or take a long pause, or even decide not to get involved at all. You second-guess yourself, and realise you're not sure what the right words are. You only know how to express exactly what you mean in your own language, which for me is Punjabi. It could be Hindi, Urdu, Arabic or another language, the one you're most comfortable speaking with your family at home. But it's definitely not the same kind of confident, effortless English you're hearing from everyone around you.

I can't even begin to tell you how many times this has happened to me. As a child, as a teen, and even now as a grown woman. I didn't know what the English word for turmeric was for the longest time. In my language it's called *haldi*, and that's all I've ever known it as. That's what I'll automatically ask for at Tesco, and they'll just stare at me in response like I'm some kind of lunatic. Same for *dhaniya* – you won't hear brown families calling it coriander, or even cilantro!

I remember being in a cooking class at school once, and of course we all had to make a dish. I came home and asked my mum what to make, and she suggested I go for *jeera aloo*. This is an Indian potato dish that's really easy and quick to make, but super delicious. I swear Indian people perfected the art of conjuring up mouth-watering food in mere minutes.

It sounded ideal to me, and I agreed. There was no way I was going to attempt anything even slightly difficult; at this point my culinary skills had only so far stretched to eggs, beans and toast.

The recipe seemed like a brilliant choice when I was at home, collecting the ingredients together and taking notes from my mum. While in the middle of doing plenty of other tasks, she found the time to scribble some instructions down with me. I genuinely became that one child at school whose paper was stained with *haldi* (I refuse to call it turmeric) – *always*.

Stains aside, though, I was confident I'd do well. Simple ingredients, easy to make, and it tastes delicious – all anyone really wants in a dish. Best idea ever.

Until I got to school.

As we got started, I slowly realised everyone else was making 'normal' dishes – kind of bland and beige, if I'm honest, but they were familiar. They all looked similar. Meanwhile, I was there putting together this bright yellow potato creation, that looked so totally unlike anything else in the room. Then I had to explain to the class and my teacher what it was. And while it was simple, it was nowhere near as simple as the sad grey vegetable soups half my classmates had mixed up.

Suddenly, *jeera aloo* didn't feel like such a great move after all. I decisively stuck out like a sore thumb – or in this case, a neon yellow thumb. If I'm honest, I didn't even know how I would describe the dish to the class. 'It's potato! Yes, I know it's bright yellow … Yes, I know you've never seen potato look like this before … Yes, I know you don't even believe me that it *is* potato … but it's really tasty, I promise!' A bit awkward, to say the least. No one else in the class had to desperately justify what they'd made in the same way. That day, I wondered if perhaps bright yellow doesn't necessarily mean a bright idea.

Straddling two completely different cultures can be tough. The strongest, most difficult part is the feeling of alienation. You don't quite belong on one side; you don't quite belong on the other. It can feel like you don't have a home, and while you drift back and forth, you're never fully accepted anywhere.

But when you really step back, it's not all bad, is it?

We brown girls certainly get to experience unique moments when we're growing up. Such as the time my siblings and I were washing our parents' car. My eldest sister was probably under the age of fifteen, which means the rest of us were definitely under ten.

Picture us: a group of little brown people, dutifully washing our parents' car, singing along to Mousse T's 'Horny' at the top of our lungs, on the driveway in shorts and vests, soaked with water and soap.

It genuinely looked like an underage wet T-shirt competition. So, *so* wrong.

We didn't know any better and, to be honest, who even knows if our parents did. But I dread to wonder what our neighbours thought!

In Bollywood, though, bursting out into song in the middle of *literally anything* is totally normal, and that's what we grew up seeing. There isn't a moment that's not ideal for a song and dance. Dropped something on the floor? Let's sing about it. Bumped into someone? Let's make it dance. Scratched an itch on your chin? Good thing there were two hundred backup dancers hidden behind that tree, because it's time for a showstopper.

As brown girls, a tendency towards a bit of drama and show is in our blood.

My parents used to enjoy Saturday nights out with their friends. They would come home afterwards, bringing everyone back with them to collect their children and to unwind for the rest of the evening with some chai and cappuccinos. (Asians love cappuccinos for some reason. I'm not sure why it's never a flat white, or a straight espresso shot? Always a cappuccino. It's like a law or something.)

As all the parents sat in our living room chatting away, I

would think it was the perfect time to show them what I'd been up to while they were out. No doubt I would have a performance ready. I would go from dancing along to a pop routine, to hip-hop (my audience usually looked absolutely clueless as to what on earth this mysterious 'rapping' was supposed to be on about), to taking it all the way to the Middle East and trying to belly-dance. For that last one, I'd got the inspiration from a holiday we took to Egypt when I was twelve, and we bought the traditional coin skirt that makes all the noise when you shake. Okay, so I probably didn't know what I was doing, but the skirt made it look like I really had some moves.

So, basically, I would do my very own spectacular one-woman show. And I didn't think anything of it.

I remember occasions like this and think, *Would this fly if we were in India?* Probably not! In India, I don't think belly-dancing is the preferred method for entertaining your parents and all their friends.

Then, on the other hand, the impulse to turn a chilled Saturday night with cappuccinos into a literal song-and-dance – is that a Western thing? I don't think so. I think that's pure Asian flamboyance.

However, find that sweet spot in between the two, and you'll get something spectacular.

Take Christmas Day. We

all celebrate it, because it's such a core part of the Western culture we've become immersed in. Plus we do all love a roast, and an excuse to buy our loved ones gifts (not to mention being given some nice presents ourselves). But for some reason, a tree and a few carols simply doesn't do it for brown families. Indians have to turn Christmas into some sort of pre-wedding party for New Year's Eve, and blast out the Bhangra and Bollywood tunes. Everyone's getting up to dance and pulling people up to join them. I have to say, we've had a few Christmases like this – some of which I really don't want to remember!

It's just another great example of how being a British Asian, straddling two cultures, isn't all that bad. There's so much good to be found in the fusion of two different worlds.

Brown Girl Problems

'When I was sixteen my mum found Smirnoff in my school bag, and I blamed it on my friend.'

Does your friend know she took the wrap? I'm thinking I would have to give my friend a heads up about it, in case she ever wanted to come to my house – because if my family believe she hid alcohol in my bag, she is definitely not welcome round any more.

Actually, not only would I never invite that friend

around ever again, but in front of my family I'd basically start pretending she didn't exist any more. Absolutely no mention of her from that day forward, because I know my mum now instantly dislikes her and categorically does not want me spending time with her. Oh, remember that friend who you used to spend every waking moment with, who you called your best friend in the universe and said you'd never lose touch with for as long as you live? Nope, no one remembers her. Never existed.

I'm not judging your tactics here at all. We have *all* done this. We have all had no shame in blaming things on our poor friends that have not a clue.

I always pick a friend who is white, or Black, or otherwise non-Asian, because my parents will be less judgemental of that friend, and it'll be less of a shock. I found it much easier to get away with this because I didn't have a lot of Asian girl mates growing up anyway; in fact, I don't even now. So it was easier to justify why my friends were behaving in a way that I claimed I never would. It's cheeky, but unfortunately it's true – they just don't get judgement in the same way as I would, and my parents are much more likely to let it go. I knew it would work, and it did, every time.

If you blame something on your friend who's a fellow brown girl, though, your mum is instantly going to take a different approach. As soon as they hear a brown girl's name, it's like something in their brain just flips. They'll automatically start interrogating you.

What's her surname? Hmm, that's a Sikh name. Where exactly does her family come from? Well, that's something you should have found out when you were first making friends. What do her parents do? What do you mean, her parents are divorced?!

They want to know every single thing about her family, so they can explain just why they're inferior and you're superior – why *that* girl would do something so shameful as drinking vodka, and why their own girl never would.

So this brown girl scapegoat will already be subject to a lot of scrutiny and judgement. Beyond this, sometimes your parents will have no trouble communicating with your fellow brown girls' parents, to let them know just what their daughter's been up to. And then that poor innocent brown girl will pretty quickly be subject to the Aunties' merciless whispers.

Brown girls aren't meant to drink. Not openly, not copiously, and especially not when they're young. But bizarrely, in some of our cultures, and especially in the Punjabi culture where I'm from, it's quite a thing.

I've grown up watching my parents have house parties almost every single weekend. I'm not talking about moderate gatherings of one or two other couples – I'm talking *big* numbers. More than a hundred guests on a casual Saturday night, no occasion necessary. If it wasn't the big house parties, they'd have a group of maybe ten couples who would come over to pre-drink, before heading out to a fancy restaurant for the evening while the kids stayed at home with the babysitter. Then they'd return even more merry than before.

I can remember being a young girl and asking my parents, 'What are you drinking?' They'd happily let me try a sip of their Bacardi and coke, or Malibu and lemonade. When you're young, drinking is fascinating (well, I guess anything that you're not supposed to do is), and I think my parents fully understood my curiosity around alcohol. They weren't afraid to let me try experiencing it, in a safe and controlled way of course.

Saying that, if I were caught at sixteen years old with a Smirnoff in my school bag, my parents wouldn't exactly be giving me a pat on the back.

The irony here is that if my parents hadn't moved to a Western country, would they even socialise in the way that they do? It's almost as if our families modify themselves in a way to better suit their environment, but want to restrict us from doing the exact same thing.

A bottle of Smirnoff in your bag is definitely 'too modern', and the Aunties or your parents will immediately start blaming Western culture for your indiscipline. What I find funny is the Aunties themselves come to live in Western countries, adapt to Western ways and sometimes become more relaxed. The Aunties will often have social lives that they might not have had back home. They'll drink, try shisha, and do all the rest, yet they'll judge young brown girls that have actually been born and raised in a Western society. It's like they believe we don't deserve to enjoy any aspects of Western life, simply because we haven't had to change or adapt to access them.

Or they'll try to justify their actions with their age: 'I'm older than you, so I know better.' Doesn't matter if you're thirteen or thirty, they *will* use this excuse. Sorry, Auntie, but I don't buy it. If it's wrong for me, it's wrong for you.

As long as we're being safe, towards others as well as towards ourselves, then we deserve to enjoy it all. Especially when the rules telling us to hold back are enforced by parents, families and Aunties who don't exactly hold back themselves.

If you get caught and need to point the finger at someone else, it can feel a bit morally dubious, I know. But it's genuinely understandable and, dare I say it, sometimes the best thing to do. Especially if the friend isn't Asian, it'll probably have no effect on them, while saving you and your parents a whole load of heartache.

So don't worry, girl. You do you.

'How do I find myself when I'm living in a brown household?'

There's finding yourself, and there's finding yourself in a brown household. These are two completely different scenarios.

Let me give you some examples.

How about . . .

You: 'I really enjoy doing art at school. I think I'm going to look into applying for some creative jobs.'

Your family: 'Art? Creative? Oh, no. Why would you like that? It doesn't pay. Don't do art.'

Or maybe . . .

You: 'I want to go travelling on my own for a year. I think it'll be an amazing chance to see the world and meet new people.'

Your family: 'No. You can't go on your own, it's not safe and you won't be able to manage. If you must go, go with your cousin.'

Ideas of what you think you like, or what you think you want to do, are tough to actually explore in a brown household. If you summon the courage to speak up about it, you'll probably be rewarded with uncertainty at best, or active discouragement at worst.

If only it were as simple as backpacking to India to 'find yourself'. Seems to be what a lot of our white friends do, doesn't it? Just imagine you told your parents you wanted to do that. Absolutely no way will they bless your journey and just request the odd postcard or two. Instead, they'll likely insist you stay with some family member you've never met, and ensure that they chaperone you everywhere you go. Daily postcards will be mandatory, to prove you're exactly where you said you'd be. The only backpacking you'll be doing is going from one family member's house to the next, for three-course meals at breakfast, lunch and dinner. Your backpack will get heavier and heavier from carting around the leftovers they forbid you from leaving without, or the unnecessary gifts they want you to take back to your family.

For me, that is pretty much what a trip to India has to be. Have I ever truly found myself visiting family, even just a little bit? Absolutely not. The only thing I've ever found on a trip to India is a pack of Imodium to settle my Delhi belly.

Our families always want what's best for us, or, at least, most families do. But they don't necessarily have the required knowledge to help us on everything. They can be quite ignorant about things going on in the world that have never concerned them. So the music career you desperately wish to embark on won't ever be encouraged – not because their fears of you having a low income or finding yourself unemployable are actually founded on anything, but purely because they know nothing about it. If they don't immediately understand how you'll get a foot in the door, or how you'll make money (and you know how important *that* is in the Asian community), then they will tend to dismiss it as a waste of time.

If you want to find yourself while living in a brown household, you have to learn to block out the uninformed, negative opinions of others and follow your heart.

It's definitely easier said than done, I know. It's especially frustrating when everyone feels they have the right to discuss your decisions or your future. Everyone thinks their opinion is vital to how you live your life.

My advice? Just smile and nod. It's much easier than arguing, and it doesn't mean you have to take their words to heart.

Then, when they've left you alone, pursue your own choices. You'll be happy with it, because you've informed yourself on everything you need to know, and you know it's the right thing for you.

You'll get by just fine.

'I made dinner for the white guy I'm dating, and he told me he doesn't want to try Indian food.'

Woah.

Firstly, I have to say it's an actual crime to not like Indian food. I am personally offended. Okay, so I haven't quite mastered cooking all the dishes just yet – but I *am* excellent at eating them! Give me the meal and I'll be able to tell you if it's a good or bad Indian; I just can't quite make it myself without my MasterChef of a mum.

A part of me feels unbelievably sorry for this young man, as he is obviously lacking serious flavour and colour in his life! Don't get me wrong, a Sunday roast with a plate full of veg sure looks enticing, but it really isn't comparable to a simple dish my mum cooks up on a Tuesday. Food is a huge part of our culture, and it's always rich in so many flavours.

If you came to my house for an afternoon tea, you would not be getting simple cold sandwiches and tea with some scones, oh no. Brown people take it a step further – *always*. There will be a plate of samosas, possibly spring rolls, some meat dishes and a selection of veg dishes, and you can't forget a huge plate of *chaat*.

Man, I'm drooling.

On a fair few occasions, my mum has casually invited people over, just as a last-minute thing, so they think it's a quick tea and a snack. Little do they know there is a five-course dining experience awaiting them, equivalent to – or, if I'm honest, better than – The Ritz. But, believe me, they always manage to tuck in anyway.

It can be a bit disheartening if you're with friends, or someone you're dating, and they don't take much interest in you and your culture. And food is arguably one of the biggest parts of brown culture. Food is love, and it's also the way we give love. We have a high standard of hospitality in our culture, and it's ingrained in us to feed (or overfeed) our guests. Sure, it's sometimes to the point where it can be a little embarrassing, but we know it's all with good intention. Feeding someone is the brown person's way of bestowing the utmost love and respect. It's a must.

No relationship can work if it's only one-way. I imagine you were at least willing to try any food he's prepared for you. And really, it's one thing to not like something if you've tried it – fair enough, you've given it a go and now you're certain it's not for you. But if you haven't even tried it, well then hey, you're missing out without even trying to learn what you're missing out on, and that's not exactly fair.

If things were to progress, how would he deal with an Auntie shoving *barfi* (Indian sweets) in his mouth at every celebration? Because, let's be real, no one gets a choice on those occasions – it's going in.

We now live in such a multi-cultural society that we all need to be accepting of everyone around us, as the bare minimum. But more so, we have to not let ourselves be content with our own ignorance, and instead actually educate ourselves on the people we know and where they come from.

My advice to you is to try to explain this to your boyfriend. If he's an understanding guy and he cares for you, then he'll push aside his reservations and try it out.

I swear, though, he might be the only white guy in the entire world that doesn't want to try Indian food. Who doesn't love a curry?

Brown Girl Wisdom

Coming from two cultures can feel like you don't have a home on either side. It may seem like you're the only person in the world who goes through all the weird, crazy situations that you do – when you're growing up, and even through your adult life. You're pulled in opposite directions all the time, and your brain's never entirely sure which way it wants to go. You're in the middle of two sides, and you're alone.

But I promise you, you're not.

Even now, as a grown woman, when I'm at a professional event or a friend's house party and I notice I'm the only brown person there, I often think things like, *Are they looking at me strangely?*; *Did I say the wrong thing, or use the wrong word?*; *Should I have kept my mouth shut?*; *'Do they all think I'm a freak?'*

I try to remind myself, though, that if I constantly think like this, I'm only causing a further divide between myself and the people around me that aren't like me. Perhaps they *do* think I'm different, but if I succumb to worrying about it, I'll just make it worse.

And anyway, no two people are completely alike. I'll

never meet anyone who's exactly like me. There will always be differences. Why concentrate on those, when we can instead focus on the many things that tie us together?

That isn't to say that those alienating experiences don't happen, out of our control. Sometimes we *are* excluded, or singled out in a group, and it can feel totally demoralising. And it's not just in Western communities, either. We might also feel a bit out of place in our own Asian communities, especially when an Auntie has glared at the G&T in our hand and hissed that it's 'too modern'. Or even when there's a clique of other brown girls giving you a dirty look when you enter the room because you're hanging out with a bunch of non-Asians. Trust me, I've been there.

However, it's up to us to show people that we're here, we are who we are, and we're open to educating them about ourselves. We can show off our beautiful culture to Western people, while also wholeheartedly embracing theirs. If we want to feel a part of the collective community, we also need to make them feel a part of our side.

And meanwhile, we can introduce the judgemental Aunties to fun 'modern' things like Netflix, or posting on Instagram, or maybe even a cheeky glass of wine. We can encourage them to understand that it doesn't mean they're abandoning their roots. We can let them know that, although they may not have been able to indulge in such things during their own youth, that doesn't mean they have to resent us for having the opportunities to do so. We all have those opportunities now, and we can enjoy them together.

We brown girls can feel like we're torn across two

different sides. But why do we have to pick a side? Can't we make a new home for ourselves in the middle?

I actually think some of our sisters back home are well ahead of us on this front. For example, I always thought girls in India definitely couldn't dress a certain way, or drink alcohol, or go clubbing, or do any of the things I was forbidden from doing. After all, that's why my parents were banning me from such activities, right? To uphold the Indian traditions?

In truth, the brown girls I see or speak to in Delhi or Mumbai are often living way cooler, uninhibited lives than a lot of us 'Westernised' brown girls. Seriously, the casual style and flair from some of them is incredible. They're all chilling out on Instagram in their glitzy, sexy outfits; meanwhile I'm trying to tug my skirt down my shins to avoid glares from the Aunties.

I wonder if our parents who had to move over to the West are deliberately stricter with us, trying to hold on to the rules and traditions that they knew back home so they don't lose their roots. It makes me think: we believe we Westernised brown girls have the most freedom of all, but actually, we have to try a lot harder to hide secrets and keep up appearances. Some of those desi girls back home would probably look at our lives in the UK and think it's a shame we have to sneak around so much.

But maybe we don't have to any more. Maybe we can all start hiding a bit less, and embracing a bit more. We need to help our parents understand what those girls back in India already know full well: adopting and enjoying parts of Western culture doesn't make us any less Asian. On the contrary, I believe the fusion of two lifestyles means we're able to bring out both of them in even sharper definition.

We are so lucky to be able to live in two cultures. Because of it, we get laughs and joys like no one else. We get the best food, the best clothes, the best music, the best films, the best technology. We get the best of both.

And it doesn't even stop there, if you ask me. These days, especially with the help of the internet, we're able to embrace all the cultures of the world, and be as one. We can all be unified in our similarities while celebrating our differences. We're one big, global community that each and every one of us can find a home within.

Sounds like an appropriately 'modern' idea to me.

5

'DON'T GO IN THE SUN'

I spent many years avoiding the sun.

I'd go on holiday with my white friends, and they'd all be so excited to get a tan. In fact, it'd be one of their central holiday goals: to get as dark as they possibly could. They would even seek out some time on sunbeds to get a tan *before* going, in order to get a better tan on the holiday. Tan squared.

I couldn't fathom how much work they were putting in just to be closer to my skin tone, something I possessed naturally and effortlessly every single day. It seemed curious to me that they were so keen to get darker, when at the exact same time, getting darker was the number-one thing for me to steer clear of.

There went my friends, going to these extreme lengths to look even a little bit darker – and there *I* was doing the complete opposite. I would strive to avoid the sun, desperate not to get any darker than my natural skin colour at all costs. It got to the point where I'd even sit away from my friends on the beach, as I'd insist on finding a spot with some shade.

Why? Because in many brown cultures, looking 'dark' isn't seen as beautiful.

It's not just something that affects the women, either. When my brother was born, he was slightly darker-skinned than my sisters and me. Although everyone was so excited to finally have a boy in our family, there was still something to pick at – his skin tone. The Aunties would make jokes that my mum might have had an affair with the milkman, because my brother looked so different to us. Continuing the dairy theme, my grandmother even suggested that my mum should make her son drink lots of milk, so his skin would get lighter. (I have to say, this method was tried and tested, and it was a certain failure. Please do not try this at home. Sure, cows are considered sacred in many Indian cultures, but milk isn't *that* magical.)

While there is obviously bigger pressure on women than on men to look conventionally attractive, the bias against dark skin gets us all. Yay for equal opportunities, I guess?

This idea that brown people need to be lighter-skinned to be considered beautiful and worthy has been the mantra for centuries. From what I understand, the roots of this mindset partly stem from slavery, classism and colonialism. Now I'm not here to provide a full history lesson, but to perhaps help you understand in less than a minute:

Being lighter-skinned was a sign of wealth in our culture, because those Indians with darker skin were more likely to have been labourers, therefore darker-skinned due to spending more time doing work outdoors and in the sun. On the other hand, the richer and more privileged families spent time in their palaces, shielded from the sun, keeping their skin light. The difference was exaggerated by the divide between north India and south India. Politics, wealth and influence were concentrated in the north, leading to the south – where people were darker, due to the hotter climate – being seen as inferior. And finally, the idea was compounded during the British Raj, when the ruling class were all fair-skinned Westerners and there was an assumption that being paler was synonymous with having more power. In essence, society's 'better' people were lighter-skinned – and it's not hard to work out what that meant for everyone else.

There you go! The entirety of South Asian colourism in a few sentences. To sum it up, it's basically a twisted take on Snow White: everyone wants to be the fairest of them all.

But the reality of colourism's effects is nothing like a children's fairy tale. The prejudice darker-skinned girls face causes a lot of harm, even today, when you'd hope we were past all those old-fashioned associations of skin colour with class and wealth.

The Bollywood film *Bala*, which came out as recently as 2019, was supposed to be a protest against colourism. But it cast a light-skinned actress and used makeup to darken her complexion, rather than casting a naturally darker woman, which would have been a much bolder statement in Bollywood's almost entirely fair-skinned world. The film's producers chose to conform to the very ideals they were supposed to be objecting to. The hypocrisy of choosing not to hire a darker-skinned woman sends a much stronger, and more worrying, message – and it overshadows anything positive that the film was supposed to say.

Worse still, many women are shunned, mocked and bullied for having darker skin. There are cruel nicknames slung at victims, and sometimes even physical attacks. When a girl has darker skin than the rest of her family, in many cases she's denounced as an outcast, and a financial burden who will never get married off. In such cases, girls may not be safe from abuse in their own homes.

Darker-skinned girls face so many problems in brown communities. Due to societal stigma, they have reduced chances of friendships, romantic relationships, employment and sometimes even basic safety. It's no wonder many women feel compelled to turn to dangerous methods of whitening their skin.

At a young, impressionable age when I was just starting to care about how I looked, adverts for products such as Fair and Lovely really stood out to me. Firstly, I was seeing a product that was aimed towards South Asian women – something I wasn't used to seeing at all. And secondly, it was rare that I ever saw anyone with my skin complexion in mainstream adverts or on TV and in magazines. The only people that we did have representing us young brown girls were Bollywood actresses, many of whom were already fair-skinned, and even they were promoting this brand. Because of that, I was even more interested in it and its messaging.

Because, fundamentally, who doesn't want to be fair and lovely?

But when you look into what products like these actually do, it's suddenly a lot more sinister than a fairy tale. Fair and Lovely (Unilever changed the name of this product to 'Glow & Lovely' in 2020 following criticism) and its competitors are skin whiteners, which means they lighten the skin in order to make it a fairer shade. This involves the use of harmful and toxic chemicals. Many of these kinds of creams, sprays, pills and injections are illegal in some countries – and the ones that aren't are still flagged for potentially causing irreversible damage to the skin.

Suddenly, being fair doesn't seem so lovely.

Despite the dangers, these products are very popular in South Asia, and with brown people across the world. And it's no wonder. Imagine a young, darker-skinned brown girl who loves the Bollywood stars. Of course she does – they're the only women who are successful and look anything like her. They're her idols, and her inspiration; she wants to be just like them when she's older.

Then those same women appear in adverts for a whitening cream. What does that tell this young girl, and all young girls? That a brown woman can only guarantee admiration and popularity if she has a lighter complexion? Are our talents, skills or education not enough to be successful, if we're not also fair-skinned?

You can see why women and girls decide to take the risk of damaging their healthy skin for ever.

It's not just us – Auntie is looking in her magic mirror and also wishing she was the fairest of them all. Maybe poor Auntie isn't actually such a wicked witch; she's just unhappy with how she sees herself. So she takes her bitterness out on the fair Snow White, by telling her not to go in the sun.

Like I said earlier, it gets us all.

With all these messages coming at us every day, learning to accept and love your natural complexion is incredibly tough. When you're a girl, it's pretty much impossible to block out – it creeps in subtly, and informs how you view the world and yourself. My skin colour is something I and probably most brown girls or women have battled with all our lives. Wondering if it's too dark, whether that mild tan you accidentally got in the summer is acceptable or not, and even wondering whether your natural tone is good enough to make you marriage material.

It took me a long time to realise how being tanned, brown, Indian, or whatever else you want to call it, makes me unique and different in the most beautiful way.

When I first started wearing makeup at around the age of seventeen, I remember going to MAC and asking for a shade or two lighter than my actual skin tone. I figured it would make my face look flawless, luminous – all the stuff I'd been told fairer women have. I thought I'd be seen as more attractive to Indian guys, too. But when I look back at the pictures now, I actually cringe. I can see how ridiculous it looked: my face was fair, and my neck was considerably darker. It looked fake, and confusing.

On the other hand, I know that as I started to love myself and my skin colour more, I wanted to deepen it further. I wanted to enhance it, bronze it, play with it, almost make it the forefront of every makeup look I did.

When I'm bronzed or tanned, this fiery red lip will look beautiful.

This gold eye makeup is really going to make my brown skin pop.

These warm highlighters shine so brightly on my tan complexion.

When I went on my first sister's hen-do to Barcelona, I was under strict orders to make sure I didn't come back 'too dark' for the wedding, and back then I was keen to obey. But by the time it was my second sister's wedding (and for all weddings and big events since), I wanted to make sure I went out of my way to look more tanned. The rebel in me just wanted to do the complete opposite of what was expected of me. Something as simple as being a few shades darker made me feel like I had a small win, like I was moving away from the old-school mentality.

Because the historic source of this colourism makes absolutely no sense. How can the shade of your skin say anything about how valuable you are as a person? Think about this: brown people believe fairer is favourable, while Western people believe a slight tan shows off your luxurious holidays in the sun. This just demonstrates that all these ideas are made up by the societies they come from – they're not real or true. They are basically meaningless.

It's only as you grow up that you can start to become more comfortable with who you are and what you look like. It takes real effort and perspective, and a conscious effort to defy the prejudices from our past. It's not easy, but you can actually learn to appreciate your complexion, your race, the tones that make you who you are.

And the more you start to accept it, it's almost as if you wear it better. When you love what you've got, you rock your complexion with more confidence.

Then you finally realise: there's really no need to be the fairest of them all.

Brown Girl Problems

'I've overheard Aunties talking about me, saying things like, "She's got nice features for a dark girl."'

What does this even mean? Last time I checked, your skin tone doesn't determine how your features look. It's not like two brown girls with a similar skin colour automatically have similar facial features too. Make it make sense, Auntie.

Unfortunately, I've heard this passing comment way too many times. You'll see a dark-skinned girl – whether they're south Indian, Sri Lankan, Black, or from any other community – and the Aunties will point it out when they see something about her that is exceptionally beautiful. She may have a look about her, a lovely smile or a twinkle in her eye, something that really captivates everyone. It won't go unnoticed, and nor should it. Of course we should celebrate the beauty of the women around us.

But the Aunties will always bring up her skin, too. And they'll always do it in a tone of surprise.

For some reason, it's believed that the darker the skin, the unlikelier it is that the woman can be beautiful. If a darker-skinned woman is deemed attractive, then it's in *spite* of their complexion, and never because of it or in addition to it. It's almost as if the 'light-skinned community' are the people who define beauty standards, and they have the authority to give out approval and acceptance to darker-skinned people. Or to withhold it.

Either way, this is not cool.

Let's think about what the Aunties even mean by 'nice' features. These ideas are generally based on a stereotypical Western image of what beauty is, such as: a small or thin nose; perfect white teeth; big eyes; a dainty bone structure; a slim figure. And, let's not forget, all of this has to be complemented by white or light skin.

These are the types of women I saw constantly when I was growing up, before social media came along. In films, on adverts, in magazines. I never saw anyone that particularly resembled me in the mainstream media, and instead, the same ideals were reinforced over and over again.

Our own parents or families will notice someone dazzling on TV and remark on how nice their nose, or hair, or smile is. You can't help but compare yourself. We forget the fact that these celebrities can pay for expensive makeup, skincare routines, nutritional plans, fitness regimes, and perhaps cosmetic surgery. Instead of accepting ourselves for the way we are, and feeling good enough, we measure ourselves against the type of people who have been placed on such a high pedestal for so many years. And we beat ourselves up because we can't attain the same levels of 'perfection' that they can – because we never talk about how unrealistic and rigid it all is.

Thankfully, the world is starting to change now. For one, we're having conversations like this, which the Aunties never could when they were young brown girls. We're able step back and analyse our beauty preferences critically, and that means we can start dismantling them.

Secondly, there are so many young women on social media proudly representing themselves for who they are, including their skin tone. The internet has allowed everyone in the world to become a public figure, if they choose – and so we're finally seeing a wide range of different people in the spotlight. We don't have to flick through a bunch of channels, struggling to find someone who looks like us. We now have the choice to follow who we want, and feel empowered as a result.

I know I may not fall into the category of 'dark-skinned', but I am a woman of colour. A colour that I was once not so proud of, and didn't believe to be beautiful. I didn't believe my features could be attractive, either.

I've never understood how we can judge someone for the way God made them. Your skin tone should never affect how you're valued. It's simply something that you're born with. It's a natural attribute, like hair colour or eye colour. It just *is*. And the exact same thing goes for someone's features. They just *are*. It makes no sense to start adding value judgements to these things, as though someone's physical appearance is an indication of their worth.

We need to educate our parents and families to not make excuses for someone's attractiveness. We can't impose a framework on beauty – there is no right or wrong way to be beautiful. Someone's dark skin does not undermine the fact that they're gorgeous.

The sentence should stop at, 'She's got nice features.' Period.

'I've had people tell me I'm too fair for an Indian. I've been fake tanning since the age of sixteen because of it.'

The irony is, although many of us are told we're too dark for a brown girl, some of us are told we're not dark enough.

Argh.

Who even made these rules up? It sometimes feels as if there's one single acceptable shade of brown, and if you're anything below or above that, you don't quite make the cut for being a true brown girl.

News flash, Auntie: you've never met anyone in your entire life who completely matches that elusive, perfect tone – and chances are, you never will.

Brown girls come in a *huge* array of shades and, personally, I love it. Actually, forget that – human beings from every race and culture come in so many different shades and tones. You don't see African people as only one tone, nor Spanish, nor Chinese. It's true for white people, too. Being part of a particular ethnicity doesn't mean everyone is a carbon copy of each other.

I remember working at MAC Cosmetics, and part of the job was to match foundation shades on customers. Although it could sometimes feel like quite a repetitive, mundane task, it was the best way to learn about skin complexion and different undertones.

If you speak the lingo, you'll know what I mean when I say I'm around an NC42 in MAC shades. So are my sisters, and so are a lot of other brown girls. In my head, that was the go-to shade, almost like a starting point for me to work from.

But when I first started doing these foundation matches on all sorts of people, with all sorts of backgrounds and undertones, I started to realise that I was putting people in categories. I had a subconscious idea of what they were 'supposed' to look like, depending on their race or ethnicity, and it was obscuring the uniqueness of their personal colours and complexion. And by putting myself in the NC42 box, I was doing the exact same thing to myself.

The more I matched people, the less I cared about guessing in my head where they were from to match their complexion correctly. Their skin tone was just their skin tone, regardless of where they were from.

The same goes for all of us brown girls.

You shouldn't have to tan your skin to look 'more Indian'. This also applies to those who are darker-skinned and feel they need to lighten their complexion. Both methods could be harmful to your skin, as well as costly. And if it's for the sake of others and what they think, then it's also a complete waste of your energy and time. This desperation to match the ideal shade is based on a limited idea of brownness – but the expansiveness and complexity of the brown experience can never be limited.

There isn't a model to follow; all South Asians don't belong in the same box. There's no one perfect shade to be a true brown girl. I, for one, am grateful for that.

'I've been told not to go in the swimming pool because the chlorine will make me darker.'

The Aunties really think they're scientists too, don't they?

I honestly wonder where they get their 'facts' from. Did someone send a message in their community WhatsApp group, forwarding on some extreme 'true' story of a person being burnt by chlorine once? Did the Aunties then decide that the moral of the story is that chlorine makes your skin darker? Seems like they did. And now it's circulating across the world.

That's usually how it goes, isn't it? They believe anything that comes from a forwarded message. Especially if it links to a website, even if it's just your Mild Auntie's personal lifestyle blog which gets three hits a month.

In fact, the Aunties pretty much believe anything an authority figure told them when they were younger. I believe it's because answering back was always deemed a sign of disrespect. Daring to ask questions would immediately be met with accusations that they were trying to make their elders look inferior. No one wants to be faced with that anger, over and over again. So the Aunties just learned to accept what their elders told them. And the more superstitious and doom-mongering the story, the more likely it is that the Aunties will take it as gospel.

In one way, I guess it's nice that there's some innocence and gullibility to them; it makes them seem just a bit childlike, which is adorable. But in other ways, they *are* grown women, and so I wonder why they've never questioned anything! Seriously, Auntie, if the chlorine thing is true, then why have all those Olympic swimmers not burned to a crisp by now?

No, the chlorine doesn't make you darker.

However, where there's an outside pool, there's probably sun. It's true that you can spend a day at the pool and wind up darker by the end, but you don't actually have to set foot in the water. You can simply float on an inflatable Lilo on top. Honestly, it's how I always get my best tans – count me in.

I remember being on holiday one summer in Egypt with my mum and siblings, just before I turned thirteen. We were staying at an all-inclusive resort and it was great for families. The best bit of all was the huge pool, with tons of kids playing around at all times.

On one of the days, my mum and sisters wanted to take some time out to plan some excursions. Problem was, my brother and I did *not* want to leave the pool. We'd already made some new friends, and we were eager to soak up every opportunity to splash around. It's not as if we get amazing weather and have a swimming pool at our disposal back at home, after all. My brother and I agreed we'd be a couple of hours and meet the rest of the family back at our room.

True to our word, a little while later we got back to our room and knocked on the door. We'd managed to completely wear ourselves out, and were ready to relax and get some dinner.

No word of a lie, my mum did not even recognise us. We'd got the darkest tans, and were literally unrecognisable for the rest of the trip.

The point is – we had the best time. If we worried about what our skin colour was going to look like by the time we got out of the pool, we probably wouldn't have had that much fun. Yes, we did get teased and laughed at by our family, but we were able to brush it off. It was a tan, and we all knew it would fade. And anyway, we genuinely looked pretty good. To be honest, I've tried getting tans like that again in my adult years and I've never been able to achieve it!

We've been told a lot of myths over the years. Our Aunties were told by their Aunties, who were told by their Aunties, and so on. We're told all sorts: that scrubbing and exfoliating our skin can make us permanently lighter-skinned, or that cutting your nails after sunset is bad luck.

More often than not, it's simply not true.

There are already way too many rules to follow in life. My advice? Jump in the pool.

Brown Girl Wisdom

I was a lot more conscious of my complexion as a teenager and young woman. Beside my skin tone, which I was keen not to tan, I was also very aware of the dark circles and hyperpigmentation around my mouth, and on some other parts of my body too. Having hyperpigmentation is extremely common for South Asians, but perhaps because of the Westernised beauty standards and Caucasian friends

I'd grown up surrounded by, it gave me a heap of insecurities over the years. I've always felt like I needed to do something about it.

I've spent so much money on eye creams, serums, not to mention the tons of makeup I've collected. There are plenty of brands that make colour correctors to cover up hyperpigmentation.

So I should condemn those brands, right? For profiting off my own insecurities?

I don't believe this is so straightforward. In my opinion, we should not point all the blame at the skincare and beauty industries for how we feel about ourselves.

I am completely against skin lightening brands, which I believe put customers at risk of actual harm. The advertising on these products, as well as their physical effects, are dangerous to young girls. But there are also other products which aren't about attaining some objectively 'better' shade. Ones which don't permanently alter and damage the skin.

The makeup and creams that I use aren't about reaching some glorious standard of perfection. Instead, they're designed to help each individual with their own, personal skin goals. Ridding the world of these brands and cosmetics isn't going to solve our problems. If we go and buy someone's products so we can feel better about ourselves, that's still a choice we make, and a choice we should be allowed to make. What matters is *why* we make that choice.

We need to start by being accepting of ourselves. If that means you want to throw your concealer away and rock the dark circles, then you should be celebrated for that. But that's not the only valid path to choose. You might decide to spend your money on treatments, and if you feel that's the route you want to go down, then no one should stand in your way.

Me? I knew my personal insecurity around my hyperpigmentation could consume me, if I let it. That was something I had to honestly accept about myself. So I decided to take control over it in a way that I felt happy with. I must say, my hyperpigmentation is one of the reasons I love makeup so much. Learning to cover it up is part of how I became such an expert.

I spent my first couple of years on YouTube wanting to be a makeup artist for 'everyone', meaning I thought and felt anyone of any skin tone and background could take inspiration from my looks. And yes, in ways, of course they can. But it was my dad who kept pushing me to create makeup looks specifically for other Indian girls.

Because he'd constantly tried to push me in the direction of being 'more Indian' all my life, initially I was determined to do the opposite. Begrudgingly, I have to admit that on this occasion, he was right. At first I couldn't see that what I have is a niche, something that other people on YouTube at the time didn't have. In fact, it was the whole reason I even started making videos – for other girls who looked like me!

We brown girls don't just have to deal with how we see ourselves, but how the Aunties see us too. The Aunties probably don't realise the impact it can have when they're complimenting you because of your fair complexion, and your sister or brother is next to you fretting with self-consciousness over their own darker tone.

I can't place all the blame on the Aunties, however. Generations upon generations of our ancestors believed, as unshakeable knowledge, that society's most respectable figures are paler, while darker people are of less value. These stereotypes about light and dark skin go back hundreds, even thousands of years, and it's not an easy thing to shake overnight.

I believe it's now about politely stopping them in their tracks and educating them on why the things they say aren't just wrong, but harmful in ways they can't imagine. The only advice I want to hear from an Auntie about my skin is when she's telling me to wear daily SPF and to moisturise. That is it.

Defying the Aunties doesn't mean we disrespect them; it just means we've come a long way since they were young, suggestible brown girls. We're able to step back and evaluate our societal standards in a way we never could before.

The hierarchies that once existed for different skin tones were based on outdated, skewed societal perceptions. In other words, they were completely made up. Those old days of classes and colonialism are long behind us. It's time to leave their ideas behind, too. We're smarter now, and kinder.

We stand alongside the bold women who fight for fairness. We stand alongside model and activist Sheerah

Ravindren, who raised awareness of the Indian film industry's colourism with #BollywoodSoWhite. We stand alongside campaigner Kavitha Emmanuel, who began the 'Dark is Beautiful' movement. We stand alongside Hetal Lakhani, who started a successful petition to get the skin tone filter option removed from India's biggest matchmaking website, Shaadi.com.

I know it can be tough for By-the-Book brown girls to mentally break away from these traditions. But I'd recommend that you take a look at your Wild West sisters, the ones who are the envy of their white friends because of their gorgeous darker tones. These brown girls are seen as a defining standard for beauty. And honestly, they are.

You are, too. We *all* are. You are beautiful, no matter what shade you are. Your skin tone is a part of you, and you should learn to love it.

6

'SHE HAS NO SHAME DRESSING LIKE THAT'

Says Miss Curvy Auntie herself.

What, exactly, is the big deal around wearing something that shows your body? It's not even about showing *off* your body, although there's certainly nothing wrong with that either. But simply showing your body at all – curves, skin, the mere hint that you're a flesh-and-blood woman – even the faintest glimpse is apparently the height of shame. Wearing something as basic as a crop top when I was younger was absolutely *not* a done thing. No point even considering it. A midriff – what's that?

Unless, of course, you're wearing a sari. Only *then* it's all right, even if you're faced with the lovely sight of all your Aunties' back rolls. Apparently, *that* is acceptable, and appealing, and dignified. The rules are pretty inconsistent, to say the least.

No matter how much you protest about how little sense it

all makes, however, having the tiniest bit of skin showing as a young brown girl is just not tolerated. My older sisters and I got the message drilled into us pretty routinely: nothing tight, nothing revealing. There was no point even buying V-neck tops, because our mum would only go and make us wear camisoles underneath so there wouldn't be even a minuscule hint of cleavage. It kind of undermined the 'sophisticated, confident woman' look we were trying to go for.

I have to say, my sisters probably had it much worse than me. Me being me, I always pushed the boundaries. No short skirts? I want them shorter. No plunge necks? That's all I'm buying. Don't get me wrong – I definitely received many sharp glances of disapproval from my parents. I think I could get away with it more, though, simply because my parents had worn themselves out with my older sisters, and by the time it came to me, they'd started to pick their battles. Anyway, I was stubborn, and I wanted my way.

But would I ever dare wear any of these boundary-pushing outfits to family occasions? Definitely not.

Frankly, I don't even wear particularly revealing clothes the vast majority of the time. I actually love wearing modest clothing too. It just depends on my mood. I believe you don't have to wear less to look more sexy or attractive; to me, covering up can be just as appealing. However, even if I'm wearing something thoroughly modest, it doesn't stop the Aunties from picking away, whether it's at the colour of my outfit, its cut, or even going as far as discussing the fabric it's made from. That's why it's so important to filter my clothes – there's Auntie-appropriate and Auntie-inappropriate.

I have separate clothes for family gatherings like barbecues, dinners and other casual events – my wardrobe follows a strict system of categorisation. I make sure I keep a supply of certain tops, ones I would never usually wear, but which are 'suitable'. This means wearing one won't result in someone saying something negative, whether it's to my face or even behind my back. These tops need to be high at the front to ensure there isn't a hint of cleavage in sight; meanwhile the skirts or dresses need to be long enough, and that's including when I'm sitting down or crossing my legs.

When I'm doing a wardrobe clear-out, I consciously decide, 'I'll keep this for a family event.' If I think about it, it's embarrassing, and I shouldn't have to do that. It's crazy to have to plan a particular way of dressing, all to please your family. But it's second nature to me, something I just do.

Why? Because wearing the 'wrong' clothes to a family get-together is simply not worth the grief.

You see, the more revealing the clothes, the more opportunity there is for a judgy Auntie to have a good, long look at you. Mild Auntie will scrutinise your shape; Spicy Auntie will announce what size she thinks you are; Hot Auntie will flat-out make disparaging comments about your weight. Whether you're deemed 'too fat' or 'too slim', someone is going to tell you.

Do the Aunties forget that they, too, were young once? In their time, they were probably restricted from wearing what they wanted. They were likely advised not to wear that bold new colour or flashy modern design. Too gaudy, too attention-seeking.

Don't they remember how frustrating that was? Don't they want young brown girls nowadays to get a choice in what they wear, and how they look, without the fear of being judged by everyone?

Apparently not. Haters.

The cycle repeats itself. And so now, it's those same Aunties who've become the finger-wagging clothing judges, all grown up and self-righteous, telling us what is and isn't acceptable to wear.

Do you think that nice ruby-red colour suits you? Well, the Aunties have a different opinion. Those are your favourite jeans? Doesn't matter – the Aunties have decided they're too tight on you. Want to wear a crop top? Ha, the Aunties aren't even going to entertain that one. Better think again.

I've never understood why young brown women get so much negativity for dressing how they want to. Especially when you consider that, growing up, we've each seen a constant parade of Bollywood stars, pouting in their teeny tiny outfits, more than just some midriff on show, cleavage unashamedly out, all while prancing around and dancing provocatively. I remember thinking, as a young girl: *If they can wear clothes like that, then why can't I? They look just like me, therefore they must come from families like mine. How come their dads let them wear that? My dad would never let me wear that.*

Why the double standard? Is it that when you 'make it', all the established morals of your family and culture go out of the window? 'You can't wear that – but *she* can, because she's famous.' I'm not quite sure what message that sends to the young girls who admire, and are easily influenced by, their favourite Bollywood stars. *If famous and successful women wear skimpy outfits, does wearing skimpy outfits help to make you famous and successful?* It's all too easy to imagine how an impressionable young brown girl might struggle to follow this confused train of thought.

I'm not trying to police what the Bollywood stars wear. Some of them genuinely have incredible style. At the end of the day, they're independent adults and they can wear what they like; more power to them. However, there's a hypocrisy in the brown community idolising these scantily clad divas, while also insisting our young girls cover up. It doesn't sit right with me.

I'm aware that things are now shifting, and we as brown girls are feeling braver about our clothing and pushing boundaries more than ever before. Some of this has even been due to the empowering influence of unapologetic Bollywood fashion icons. Together, we're all challenging those old-fashioned notions around clothing, not just by speaking out, but also simply by actively doing what we want without the fear of shame. It's not just me wearing those slightly shorter skirts or slightly lower-cut tops. All over the world, Wild West and On-the-Fence brown girls are now wearing clothes we would never even have dreamed of fifty years ago. Probably not even twenty years ago. And our By-the-Book sisters are taking Asian fashion to daring new places, with brighter colours and innovative styles. It's been a slow and subtle revolution, but it's a revolution nonetheless.

Don't get me wrong – I still have my moments. When I'm getting ready to attend a family gathering of some sort, there's still a persistent little voice in the back of my head, asking me if I'm *sure* I should wear what I'm wearing.

The best thing is, I've learned how to switch that voice off sometimes. I remind myself that 'Are you *sure* you should wear that?' is the same kind of snide comment an Auntie might make. And so, I decide – yes, I *am* sure.

It's not about shocking the Aunties or causing a stir; doing something solely to provoke a reaction really isn't my style. But if the clothing is comfortable, and feels like me, then that's what I choose to wear. I also think, sometimes, that wearing family-appropriate clothes isn't necessarily such a bad thing. You don't need it all out to prove a point to your family – there are other ways of doing that, while keeping some dignity. You can push boundaries without upsetting everyone around you.

Let's forget about clothing for a second, though. Because it's not just your outfit that will get analysed and insulted.

I sometimes feel there are unwritten rules to follow on how to look, and they affect everything: wearing the 'right' clothes, being the 'right' weight, and even something as inconsequential as wearing your hair the 'right' way. Every single facet of your appearance seems to be subject to some unknown standard of what the Aunties think looks good. Or your parents, or that over-protective big brother, or that By-the-Book little sister who's still really cautious about what other people might say.

Who's ever been on the receiving end of comments about their makeup being 'too dark' – meaning you have too much on? Or have you ever been told you shouldn't wear red lipstick before you're married? I have. Of course, the rebel in me immediately goes and puts on the darkest red lip I own. Only after I'm married, you say? Ha!

Or, as another example, my whole life I've had curly hair. There've been a number of times I've heard people say it looks messy, or that straight hair looks better. I've even heard people say that a woman having curly hair makes her look like a witch.

A witch? Really? Don't say anything like that again, Auntie, or I'll put a curse on you.

Obviously, the accusation that I looked like some evil supernatural creature got to me, just a little. Growing up, I straightened my hair to death. I can't even tell you how many hours of my life I lost trying to tame the mane, all to look more like everyone else.

It was only in my adult years that I finally started to accept what I naturally had. And yes, at first, my frizzy curls with absolutely no shape or pattern may have been a bit messy, but I learned how to bring out the beauty in what I have. I did that by deciding to block out the judgement, and instead concentrate on me being me. And boy, I'm glad I did.

What does it even matter how I wear my hair, anyway? I

don't go around telling the Aunties that their bobs, buns and backcombs all look the same.

Speaking of hair, I grew up with arms as hairy as a baby gorilla – my brother can vouch for me on that – and a lot of my teenage years were spent trying to reduce that hair. If I wasn't over-plucking my brow hairs, I was finding wax strips and removing upper lip hair. My sisters and I would each sneak a turn at our mum's razor so we could go over our arms and legs.

Without a doubt, wherever you went, there was always an Auntie there to offer her waxing or threading services from home, even if you didn't ask for it! If you didn't have any insecurity about your body hair when you arrived, you certainly left with it.

I've been going to get my eyebrows threaded since the age of fourteen, and it's a biweekly ritual – a must. The worst is when you go to your local salon and the Auntie (yes, the eyebrow lady is also a random Auntie) asks if you've also come in to get your upper lip hair removed. You immediately say yes, trying to hide your embarrassment that she's even noticed it.

How are we meant to accept our naturally hairy selves when the Aunties are constantly reinforcing the notion that, without that hair, we're more beautiful and desirable.

On the other hand, I do dread to think what Auntie's bikini line looks like, and for more than the obvious reason. I'm pretty sure that's an area she's not so keen on looking after. And if you dare tell the Aunties that you maintain your lady area, there's only one thing they'll think of. Of course they won't accept that you just want to look after yourself, and maybe this is something you do for you. No such thing in the eyes of an Auntie. No, clearly, you're only doing it for someone else to see – oh, the *shame*. All of a sudden, your body hair is no longer the Aunties' biggest concern about you.

A lot of us are naturally hairy. It's simply the way we're made. But knowing that doesn't necessarily make it easier to come to terms with. It's tough to even just let it be.

We're constantly pushed towards a certain beauty stand-ard. Not just by wider society; the Aunties themselves have their own, very particular vision of what beauty is. They'll be the first to tell you to spend hundreds of pounds getting laser hair removal and beauty treatments, rather than just accepting you for who you are.

Maybe the Aunties will never fully accept us. Maybe they'll always find something about the way we look to pick on. Rather than trying to change their ways, maybe we should instead learn how to accept ourselves.

We're brown, we're hairy and we're beautiful!

Brown Girl Problems

'An Auntie told me to get a breast reduction because no one will marry me if I have double Ds.'

First of all – Auntie, are you paying for this surgery? No? I didn't think so.

Surgery! That is extreme. Just because *you* don't like *my* body, I have to resort to an expensive cosmetic procedure to completely alter it?

What if I like my double Ds? What if they're the one thing that makes me feel sexy and confident? Maybe you don't understand this, Auntie, but I'm proud to have them. I've grown up with this body, and these boobs, and they're a part of who I am. Without them, I might not even feel entirely like me any more. This is the body I use to navigate the world, and I happen to like it.

Let's turn this around and think about it from a different perspective for a moment. If I were what some call 'flat-chested', would you encourage me to have surgery to get bigger breasts? I think not. That's because you would assume I wanted to do it to look more physically appealing to men, and that motivation is totally frowned upon. However, it seems that having natural double Ds is also something to be ashamed of – and reducing them in order to attract a future husband is, apparently, fine. But don't reduce them *too* much, because you don't want to put off the men by looking too 'boyish', after all.

Erm. What?

No matter your chest size, Auntie will never let it be. Auntie will never let *anything* be. There's always something to pick on. It seems that every facet of our bodies is subject to the same criticism. And every single time, it's futile to try to achieve the perfection the Aunties are insisting on.

Weight is the most common example. Brown families are feeders. Hospitality is number one in our culture, and it's important that we provide sustenance to our guests.

If you refuse the food you're offered at Auntie's house, or only pick at a little bit of it, it'll be considered the height of rudeness. But if you go ahead and indulge in a little more than they'd like, you're slandered for it. Give it five minutes and there'll be gossip about you eating too much circulating around the community.

Whenever you meet an Auntie, she's guaranteed to comment on your weight loss or gain since she last saw you, whether or not it's even real (sometimes it's entirely in their heads). I swear I've been to events where one Auntie's told me I've lost weight, then another Auntie half an hour later has told me I've gained a few pounds. Either way, it's never a good thing. It's always something they're deeply concerned about, and they think you should be concerned as well.

That particularly image-conscious Mild Auntie won't try to hide that she's constantly aware of her *own* weight. You're guaranteed to overhear an innocent little, 'This sari makes me look huge!' or 'I can't have another slice of cake, I'm watching my figure.'

She's probably had her own Aunties poke and prod at her in the past. Telling her that no man is going to want her at her size. Unfortunately, this Mild Auntie was never taught that a man could love her or want to be with her for herself, and not just how much she weighs. So, in turn, we brown girls are encouraged to fit our physicality into the mould of a wife and mother. If we're even a gram above or below the allegedly perfect weight, we will be told about it in no uncertain terms.

I know I've always been very aware of my weight, and

to be honest I don't always speak very kindly about myself. In my family, and many Asian families, making critiques about our weight has become a standard conversational topic. But we forget that with each harsh comment we make, even if it's directed at ourselves, we're furthering a harmful message for society as a whole.

There's no such thing as a perfect body. You may have lost your target five pounds, but you'll still feel down about yourself if you overhear your skinnier cousin lamenting how bloated she looks today. It can be distressing, demoralising, and some brown girls develop huge insecurities and even eating disorders as a result.

This is why it's so, so important to be mindful of others, and to watch the comments that we make. That goes double for you, Auntie. Please, stop making comments about everyone's weight. Okay? Okay.

Oh, but the Aunties aren't just concerned about your weight. Oh, no. Your height's wrong, too.

Are you taller than average? The Aunties will shake their heads and sigh, and say you'll never get a man because you're taller than them all. Make sure to wear flat shoes.

Are you shorter than average? What a shame, you look far too young and childish. Here are some heels for you. Wear them at all times.

I fall into the petite category. My mum is petite, so are my sisters – the lot of us in fact. We're the shortest family out of all our extended families, and not only is it noticed, but everyone's desperate to make sure *we've* noticed too. No doubt, at the family gathering, someone will measure themselves against you every time they see you – despite knowing neither of you has magically managed to grow an inch since you saw each other last month. Or, when they bend down to hug you, there's always a little height comment thrown in for free. Boring.

My mum has spent her whole life wearing heels, because she's seen her height as not being attractive. The Aunties never failed to tell her how she small is. When you initially think there's nothing wrong with you, everyone telling you otherwise is bound to make you get a complex about it! It's an unwinnable game.

There's always someone waiting and ready to pick you apart. Chest size? Too big, or too small. Weight? Too big, or too small. Height? Too big, or too small. Everything is too big, or too small – it's never quite good enough.

Why? Why can no one ever be 'just right'?

I don't believe it's really about physical traits at all – it's about tearing down confidence. Brown women aren't supposed to be proud or at ease in themselves. The idealised wife is the opposite: meek, shy and eager to please. Perhaps the Aunties think our egos would swell up too much if we weren't taken down a peg or two once in a while. As a result, none of us is allowed to believe we're perfect as we are.

Hey, don't get me wrong, I believe in the importance of humility. But I don't believe we need to be bullied and insulted.

Everyone is always so concerned with our appearance and shape, and feel they can openly express their opinions about how we look, whenever they want. You could be having a day where you feel great about yourself. You could be nearing the end of a long journey of self-love and acceptance, which is not easy. You could finally be getting to the point when you're happy with how you look. Then a random Auntie picks that day to dish out her unwanted opinion. Suddenly, you're not feeling so good.

It's cruel, it's unfair, and it's selfish. Auntie has no right to charge in and start applying her own ridiculous standards to your body. You shouldn't have to do anything, and most certainly not something as extreme as surgery, so that someone will marry you. Anyone who's worthy of marrying you will appreciate and respect your body just as much as you do.

There's only one good reason to consider cosmetic surgery, and that's if you genuinely want it for yourself. Not for Auntie, not for a man, but for *you*.

I can assure you: your double Ds are a blessing. I think your Auntie might just be a hater.

'I'm nineteen in a brown household and trying to be confident and positive while having acne.'

'What's happened to your face?'
 'What did you do?'
 'Why haven't you put some makeup on?'
Some Aunties, especially the Hot ones, have no shame in asking you these questions. They do it so directly – there's

never any attempt to be tactful or subtle about it. It's as if they think you haven't already noticed you have a spot or two.

Whereas I'm pretty sure you will have looked in the mirror that day and noticed that your skin isn't exactly where you want it to be. You're already feeling self-conscious and extremely aware of how you look and so the last thing you need is some Auntie bluntly pointing it out in front of your whole family.

I suffer quite badly from really dark pigmentation and scarring from breakouts. It especially happened when I was younger, and I was so conscious and aware of it. It was the only thing I could see when I looked in the mirror.

It would always be the moment when I finally thought it had started to fade away a little, or wasn't as noticeable. *That* was when an Auntie would swoop in and outright ask me what had happened to my face. *What's happened to my face?! You tell me, Auntie! You've got two eyes, and you can clearly see it can't be anything but acne scarring. Yet you want me to answer you, in front of everyone, and force them all to bring their attention to something I was trying to hide. Thanks.*

That same Auntie then smugly bragged about how clear her daughter's skin was, because she drinks so much water. Again, not helpful. I also drink water, Auntie – I think you'll find most humans do.

It's just insensitive. It's almost as if they have no filter, and they don't process what they're about to say in their minds before it comes spewing out of their mouths. The irony is that everyone else – well, certainly us brown girls – has to be so careful and mindful of how they speak, especially around the Aunties. It's not even necessarily about what we say directly to them; we're also aware of how we speak in front of them. If there's an Auntie in the room, in the house, or basically in the local area, we have to watch what we say. My brain is usually working overtime, going at a hundred miles an hour, all to ensure I don't give myself a bad name in case I accidentally say the wrong thing. Believe me, it could happen in a second. It could happen with a single word. So why are they allowed to say what they want, when they want?

I know it's so much easier said than done, but try to block out the negativity, and think more about what can bring you positivity. Focus on you, and on growing your self-love and self-acceptance. There are so many videos to easily access online, not only on building your confidence but on how to apply makeup to cover your acne scars, or even skincare routines you can use to help get rid of it completely. I may know someone who creates tons of helpful makeup videos, *hint hint*.

Remember, though, you should never feel like you *need* to cover up anything for the sake of others. Luckily there are so many inspiring and beautiful people online to look up to. People like Sheerah Ravindren, who embraces her skin tone and the fact that she's a hairy brown girl, like most of us are. Or there's Harnaam Kaur – she has polycystic ovary syndrome, which caused her to grow facial hair that she couldn't control, and she's spoken loads on how she learned to love it and herself. And we can't forget Nabela Noor, who has dealt with a lot of negativity due to her hyperpigmentation and her weight, but has used that negativity to motivate her and not let the haters stop her dreams. I really recommend looking up these incredible women, who can help motivate and encourage you to be proud of who you are, 'flaws' and all.

I totally understand it isn't easy being your most assured self when you don't feel it deep down. Having the people closest to you make pointless remarks definitely doesn't help.

Try to tune out or reduce the impact critical voices have on you. To do this, sometimes I prepare for the worst. I imagine all the cruel questions or comments Auntie might want to fire at me that day. If, by chance, she's nice to be around on that particular occasion, then it's a pleasant and welcome surprise!

But if she's not so nice, then at least I'm braced for what's coming – and, to be honest, it's never quite as bad as the horrors I've prepared myself to expect. Instead, it just comes across as a bit silly, and petty. That makes it much easier to ignore. However, sometimes no matter how much we prep ourselves for a situation, there might always be one Auntie that says something that can completely catch us off guard with a pointless comment or nosy question. I've been there, and in those situations I find it helpful to choose how I want to respond or react. I could easily allow myself to get irritated or upset and possibly even show that in my response – the Aunties would thrive off a negative reaction. Or I can *choose* to let it go in one ear and out the other and not allow the words of someone else to affect me or change my mood. Remind yourself quietly in your head that you want to enjoy yourself, you want to be happy, you don't care what they say and I promise, all of sudden it will feel so much easier to tune out the negativity as you have the choice, and you have chosen how someone else's words or actions are going to affect you.

If you are able to turn a blind eye to the negativity, you will have more breathing space to explore what makes *you* feel good. Instead of asking your friends whether they think your nose is too big, you can have conversations about the things you're interested in. Instead of searching online for fad diet tips, you can make up dance routines with your cousins and have a laugh. Instead of spending hours agonising over which colours suit you best, you can use the time for self-care and relaxation, exploring the things you enjoy and that make you feel good.

After all, with the confidence they have to go barging around into everyone else's business, it doesn't seem like the Aunties spend much time worrying about how we perceive *them*. In their own way, they've mastered the art of blocking out negativity. I bet the Aunties have tons of advice on how they've tuned out nagging parents, and critical friends, and even their own Aunties – not to mention their husbands every now and then!

Maybe, just maybe, we could learn something from them.

'My mum accidentally saw my nipple piercings, but I convinced her that they were gems.'

Nothing to see here, just a couple of bindis stuck on my nipples, Mum – totally normal!

I can't get over the explanation you came up with. I'm

imagining that you're my daughter and I just caught you with 'gems' on your nipples. I think I'd be wondering for days why on earth you had them stuck there. Did you secretly become a cabaret dancer? Will you have tassels swinging from your nipples next? There would be *so many* questions running through my head.

I mean, I'm not even your mum and I'm overthinking this.

What if you aren't wearing a bra? Won't your mum see the piercings through your top?

What if she sees them again? She won't think these are 'permanent gems', surely?

Wait a second . . . how did she accidentally see your nipples in the first place?!

Yeah. I'm overthinking this.

Piercings anywhere other than your earlobes and your nose are most definitely considered rebellious, off the rails, outrageous. A girl who decided to get an unconventional piercing is seen as totally out of control – and, for some reason, people even say it shows that she must be spoilt. Piercings, therefore, equal spoilt. Weird, I know.

The same goes for having tattoos. They're not any more acceptable – if anything, they're considered to be even worse. Unless, of course, you're a boy and you're getting lions and other religious symbols inked all the way up your arms. That's totally okay. Even if it looks hideous. (Yes, I'm throwing a little shade here – don't mind me.)

Since I was a young girl, I've been into piercings, or other ways of decorating my skin and body to make me look more unique. Well, that's how I think of it. As a young girl, I would stick little gemmed bindis onto my nose to see how it would look if I had my nose pierced later down the line. At one point I even had these little plastic rings that would attach onto my nostril, to see how nose rings would look – and I loved them.

Sometimes, a certain look or style just really appeals to you, and you can't quite explain why. My mum and older sisters didn't have any piercings of the sort, so I'm pretty sure I wasn't influenced by them. I think it was probably the many Bollywood actresses I saw on TV and in magazines. I always noticed how their nose pin or nose ring glimmered in the light. It caught my eye every time, without fail. I was entranced by the idea of one day having that little touch of glamour myself.

I was fifteen when I first got my nose pierced. It was during my summer holidays, and we were going on a trip to visit family in India. I worked up the courage to ask my mum if I could have it done when we were there, and, somehow, she agreed that a teeny little stud would look lovely. It became the only other piercing I had other than my earlobes, and I have to say I was utterly obsessed. I loved how a small and simple embellishment could make me feel more beautiful and confident.

At around the age of sixteen or seventeen, my fascination with adorning my body with new piercings and bits of jewellery continued. I would save up the money I'd made from my part-time jobs and head to my local high street after college. I'd plan to get one more tiny piercing to my ear at a time. Just one more.

By the time I had a visibly growing collection of piercings on my ears, I was definitely too scared to come home bragging and showing them off. Instead, I'd just kind of sidle into the house, head down. I wasn't going to stop getting them, but I didn't want to rub it in, either. I remember on one of the days, I came home and my parents were having a barbecue with guests – I'd hit the jackpot! You know, for *sure*, that no one is going to kick up drama about your piercings in front of guests!

But my mum noticed I had a new one, and I received the ultimate death stare. 'No more,' she said.

I have so many more now. Every time, she still says the same thing. She's dropped the death stare now though, luckily.

But anyway, going back to you hiding your nipple piercings, I have to say I totally understand why.

Once I actually went to a piercing shop to get my own nipple pierced, believe it or not. I was feeling brave and adventurous, as teenagers often do. But as I stood there in the piercing parlour, waiting to hear if they'd go ahead or not, I was getting flashbacks of my mum's death stare. I seriously saw her death-staring at me every time I blinked.

They turned me down, as I was underage. And thank *God* – I would have instantly regretted it. I knew it'd be so much worse than a death stare and 'no more' if she saw this one.

As time went by, I eventually got my navel pierced, and my dad happened to see that at a dance performance. This was, clearly, the end of the road. I remember him calling me and telling me I had twenty-four hours to enjoy it as I'd have to take it out after that.

I think he forgot, as it's now been over ten years and I

still have it. And let's not mention the tattoos I've collected along the way and have had to keep a little secret too. *Shh.*

Clearly, no harm done. And at the end of the day, your nipple piercings don't do any harm either, and you shouldn't feel bad about having them.

Tattoos, piercings and general adornment are often frowned upon. I believe the Aunties and even the Uncles think it looks tasteless and tacky. It might not be the most respectable way of looking – well, certainly not to my family, anyway – and if you're more of a By-the-Book brown girl then maybe it's not the way for you. That's totally fair.

I do think there's a bit of a contradiction though because, traditionally, smaller piercings and some tattoos were seen as pretty normal in Asian culture. I've seen old ladies with gold hoops all the way up their ears, tiny tattoos on their hands, or permanent dots on their faces.

Just imagine if I were to do the same. Do the same rules apply?

In my opinion, it's a personal thing – just like any decisions around appearance and style. To me, these adornments are a beautiful way of making yourself unique. Yes, you have to go through a bit of pain, but once you get past that, I think they look stunning. If you want to do something to make yourself feel more confident or stand out, then that should be your choice. I think there's something genuinely incredible about creating art with your body as the canvas.

When I've shown my parents my tattoos, they've asked me about what they're going to look like when I'm much older and wrinkly. But I think, who cares at that point?!

Each piercing or tattoo marks a moment or a memory for me. It's an opportunity to share a story.

As for your nipple piercing, good on you for doing what you want to do. It's just a shame we have to lie and hide such things from our parents, as they aren't so accepting.

Just be careful with the nip slips in future, sis!

Brown Girl Wisdom

Beauty is subjective.

What the Aunties deem to be beautiful can be completely different to what young brown girls see. This probably explains why I don't find an Auntie's son attractive, although she has nothing but rave reviews for him.

Even the Hot Aunties see beauty differently to the Mild Aunties. One of them will go swooning over some black-and-white footage of a Bollywood stud from the 1950s, while another only has eyes for Shah Rukh Khan. When it comes to judging fellow women, a Mild or Spicy Auntie may tolerate a cheeky piercing or two – but Hot Auntie is having none of it.

Clearly, none of these supposed standards are real. There'll never be something that all the Aunties agree on.

If we all see something differently, why should we even take into consideration someone else's opinion of us? Why should we agonise over the things they think will make us look beautiful? It's especially true if we're modifying how we look with the sole intention of attracting or impressing a man. We're taught, pretty much all our lives, that if we don't conform to a particular ideal, we won't be suitable candidates for marriage. We won't be 'chosen'. But satisfying someone else's needs or desires should never be the end goal.

We girls are taught to wax our body hair, go on numerous fad diets to lose weight, and wear clothing that doesn't feel like a reflection of ourselves. Why is it always *us* having to strive, and change ourselves, and conform? Why don't the Aunties teach their sons to love and accept us for who we are, and not what we look like?

Aside from the idea of looking good in pursuit of attracting a husband, the competition between brown girls can also be a lot of pressure. We see it with the older generations. So much gossip over who's wearing what, or who's got the latest handbag. Instead of lifting each other up, we're constantly trying to outdo and impress each other. No wonder weddings feel like everyone is trying to keep up with everyone else around them.

I understand this isn't just the South Asian community. This is a common part of global society today, especially with social media being so present in all our lives. That includes the Aunties – they're rocking the filters, even more so than their young daughters. A lot of us don't think about the harm it can cause, and the perception of beauty we're warping with every blemish we airbrush out.

Perfection isn't realistic – it's not real at all. We need to stop pretending it is. We have to do and be better for each other, as a community. True beauty isn't about looking good for the sake of others. It's about looking good the way you feel happiest.

I have had cosmetic surgery on my nose. Throughout

my life, I was forced to hear Aunties make comments like, 'You're so beautiful, but if you just fixed your nose you'd look even better.' As a result, I found it difficult to live with. I always hated it, and couldn't accept what I had.

When I was carrying out research to see what other ethnic noses looked like after surgery, I couldn't find any. Why? Because nobody in the brown community talks about it. There are so many Bollywood stars who have had surgery, or at least a little bit of filler and Botox here and there, but it just isn't normalised. I believe it all comes down to the fear of people judging you. Everyone is quick to jump to conclusions about the decisions you make, well before they know all the facts.

So I decided: I want people to know all the facts.

When I told my dad that I was going to vlog my experience, out of worry he immediately told me not to. He thought it would open me up to abuse and criticism. My feeling, though, was that surgery and enhancements are such taboo topics precisely *because* people don't talk about them enough. I wanted to be open and honest, because my procedure was nothing to be ashamed of.

I'm so glad I did vlog about it. I got such positive feedback and gratitude from people for demystifying the process – as well as for demonstrating how empowering it could be. Yes, part of my feelings towards my nose were related to the negative remarks I'd heard in my life, but I know in my heart that I got the procedure done for *me*. Not for the Aunties, not for my family, not for some future husband. It was never about what reactions I might get from anyone else going forward. I will never again care what any Auntie may say about my nose. Because I know it was for me, and me alone.

It took a lot of reflection and self-discovery, but I knew getting the surgery was a step I could take for myself, to gain some control and to ease a worry I'd had for all my life. I've never regretted it. For me, it was the right choice, and it's helped me get closer than ever to real contentment with myself.

Learning to accept ourselves and how we look can be a long, difficult journey. Is anyone in life truly, 100 per cent happy with their looks? Probably only a complete narcissist. The rest of us sadly often experience doubts, and self-criticism, and anxiety that we aren't good enough.

But what is 'good enough'? One thing I've learned as a makeup artist is that everyone, genuinely everyone, can look completely and utterly beautiful, but it's not about what's on the outside. It's not about sticking to particular standards or following a certain style. It's about bringing out the beauty that lies within us all, and staying true to ourselves. Makeup doesn't create something new – the best it can do is help to emphasise the beauty already inside you. Your joy, your humour, your love, shown through a wide smile or an eye twinkle. After all, that's what true beauty is.

Rather than looking at our appearance and picking at

it, we have to love who we are. It's only then we learn not to worry about validation from others, whether that's your parents at home, the Aunties at a family event, or even strangers online.

It starts from the inside. It's about being unapologetically *you*.

But how?

These are my recommendations:

Write down a list of personality traits you love about yourself. Maybe you're kind, and always there to help a friend. Maybe you've got a brilliant sense of humour and always make people laugh. Maybe you're really smart, and are great at solving problems. Write them all down. Don't just think about them – put them on a piece of paper, so they're real.

Now, write down a list of your talents and skills. Are you a brilliant singer? Write it down. Are you really good at remembering scientific facts? Write it down. There are so many things you do really well, and you deserve to see all of them right there in front of you.

Finally, write down a list of physical features you love about yourself. I know it can be hard, but you have just as much going for you in this area as you did in the two above. We all do. We all possess inner and outer beauty, and our inner qualities make our features shine. Write down that you've got beautiful sparkly eyes, or shoulders that make you look stunning in a strappy dress. Remember all those times someone said they wished they had hair like yours, or skin like yours, or a figure like yours. Write them down. Do you secretly think you have nice toes? Write it down!

Keep these lists somewhere safe, and read them often.

Seeing all your amazing qualities written in front of you is a way of validating yourself, and growing more sure of the things you like about yourself. When you know yourself truly, no one can tell you anything different.

You know you; you know the best things about yourself. And, hey, nobody's perfect, so maybe even write down some of the things you want to improve on. Be careful, mind, not to use this as an excuse to beat yourself up or list loads of your perceived 'failings'. You should include more things on your positive lists than on your list of things you think you could improve on! What you're essentially doing here is a form of journaling, which is a tried-and-tested technique used by therapists. It's a great way of accepting yourself, validating yourself, and not letting other people's opinions or comments shift the way you see yourself.

Just make sure these things are coming from you, and not anyone else. You're the expert on you. It's you who lives with yourself, it's you who spends the most time with yourself, and it's you who sees yourself in the mirror every day – no one else.

And believe me, once you've tapped into that self-acceptance, your beauty will shine for the entire world to see.

7

'GET A PROPER JOB'

'Mum, Dad, my school tells me I'm a brilliant painter, and I love doing it so much. Can I go and study art at university?'

'I want to get a volunteering job for a while, and give something back to the world. What do you think?'

'I'm really grateful for the dance lessons you've paid for over the years. My school teacher says I'm good enough to go pro – can I apply to study at the dance college nearby?'

Hmm, some interesting questions being asked here. Forgive me for losing my poise for a moment, but: *hahahaha!!!*

Painting? Why would you want to go and do that? Who makes money doing art? Painting and drawing and all those things might, *might*, be a fun way for you to spend your spare time, but once you're at university and you're studying to be a doctor or an engineer or an accountant, you won't have any spare time anyway. You'll be working too hard on learning, and making sure you pass your exams. So you might as well forget about all those silly things now. Oh, all right, if you *really* feel so strongly about art, we'll buy you a nice painting as a graduation present. You can hang it up in your office at your first job. Okay?

Volunteering? Now that is just ridiculous. You'll never get anywhere by volunteering. Look at your Uncle. He owns his own business. He lives in a nice big house. He bought a new BMW last month. Yes, I know it's bright yellow and he looks ridiculous in it – money can't buy taste. But it *can* buy BMWs. Do you think your Uncle ever wasted his time volunteering? No. We never had the luxury of volunteering, after all. We had to keep a roof over our heads, and pay the bills. When your Uncle was young, he studied, and when he was older, he worked for money. Now he's stable and secure. He deserves his ugly BMW.

A dancer? You can't be serious. Look, we can all have a laugh and a joke and a dance from time to time. Your cousin likes to do her little dancing videos on TikTok, and we all enjoy them. It's just a bit of fun, isn't it? But it's hardly a respectable way to spend your life. It's great you enjoy dancing, and we're proud you're so good at it, but that doesn't mean you need to throw your future away because of it. We only got you those dance lessons so you can show off what a well-rounded person you are on your university applications. Once you've got your place to study at Oxford or Cambridge, you'll never need to dance again.

Phew! Wow, I'm sorry about that. I think I started channelling all the Aunties at once, Mild *and* Spicy *and* Hot, just for a minute there. Don't worry, I'm back to myself now.

I hope you understand I wasn't being serious in the

slightest. I'm a professional makeup artist, who films vlogs, runs a podcast and is writing a book. I'm obviously not against creative careers *at all*. I deeply appreciate the importance of artistic expression, and I know first-hand how valuable it is to spend time doing the things you love, even if they're unpaid.

But the Aunties, and many of our parents, thoroughly disagree. And while I, personally, may think all of the above is a ridiculous way to think, it's sadly what the majority of brown girls – and even boys – are going to be faced with when they're growing up. How you spend your time needs to be directly beneficial to your chances of getting employed. That's the essence of it.

Are you thinking about taking a gap year, to go back-packing and explore more of the world? Well, if you're a brown girl, you won't be allowed to unless you're married, so stop dreaming. It was certainly something I was never able to consider, sadly. It's just not the done thing, even for young men. My brother did manage to do it, but it took a *whole* lot of convincing, as our dad really detested the idea to begin with. He thought it would be a waste of time.

How did we convince my dad, in the end? We told him that it'd look great on my brother's CV.

It's all about making sure you're on the path to getting a job. And not just any job, either. The attitude many Asian families have towards medicine, accounting, law and those sorts of roles is the complete opposite of how they view pursuing anything artistic or cultural. The prevailing opinion is that, unless you're taking up an established profession, it's not a real job. Even if you're not in a creative industry and you have a stable, nine-to-five job, if it isn't any of the professions listed above, the Aunties still won't know what you actually do and maybe your job isn't worth the time either! Marketing – what's that? A producer – what does that mean? A talent agent – you've definitely lost the Aunties there.

What constitutes a 'real job', anyway?

We know it's not just about working hard. Think about that struggling actor or singer or filmmaker you know. They work incredibly hard for their art, even when it's not yet working out. But an Auntie isn't going to consider their work a 'real job'.

And we *know* it's not just about doing something you love. Ha. Get real. No way is Auntie going to entertain that one.

No, a 'real job' is all about money. A stable flow of income.

We all know some of those brown boys, don't we? The ones who love to show off their wealth, like it's their entire personality. The ones who buy a giant house, then decorate it with the most gaudy gold wallpaper and furniture – because it looks expensive, even if it doesn't look very nice. The ones rocking a Rolex, taking any excuse to roll up their sleeve so they can flash it your way. The ones in their bright yellow BMWs.

Where does it all originate? Are brown people just really, really shallow?

Of course not. Well, maybe some are, but that's no different to people in general – it's nothing to do with being brown.

When many of our families came to the West, they had nothing. Some were fleeing violence and persecution in South Asia or East Africa. They escaped to places like

Britain for a safe haven. But they had nothing. They may have been influential and well-off where they came from, but here, they had to build from the ground up. So they genuinely didn't have the time to do things like volunteering, or taking the risk of pursuing an artistic passion when it was unlikely to make any income, or certainly to start with. Money was important – not to show off or to live a life of luxury, but to be able to live at all.

I won't lie, some professions really are more reliable than others. Anyone working as a writer, or a musician, or a photographer will be happy to tell you that, sometimes, it can be difficult to find a gig, or get your work funded. Whereas there's no shortage of demand for doctors, dentists, engineers or actuaries. So, yes, the Aunties aren't entirely wrong. Following one of the more traditional professions comes with a lot less financial risk.

But for some of us, it comes with another risk. The risk of unhappiness. The risk of burning out as you try to force yourself into a position you're not suited to. The risk of trying to follow your head over your heart, and ending up miserable.

I'm not an academic person. I'm far from being an idiot, don't get me wrong, but the intensity of cramming facts I don't care about, all to pass pressurised exams that then get me a qualification in a subject I don't even like ... well, I found it hard to feel motivated by that. I really did try, for many years, but it was a constant struggle trying to fit myself into a mould I'm just not made for.

When I finally had my epiphany and decided to pursue makeup artistry, everything changed for me. I still had to work really hard, but this time I *wanted* to – and that made me work even harder. It included a lot of learning through jobs which were less well paid, or sometimes not paid at all. It involved shadowing artists I aspired to be like, learning their ways of working, and doing shifts on makeup counters to get more hands-on experience.

Building my new career necessitated taking risks. I put every penny of the little I earned back into my job. Money went towards buying new equipment, like cameras and lighting, trying to create a home studio on a budget. There was a lot of trial and error – if you don't get the set-up just right, you have to try again. On top of that, I was keeping up with all the exciting new makeup launches, constantly ensuring my knowledge and skills were up-to-date.

Basically, I spent a whole load of time, effort and money filming videos I wasn't even sure anyone would ever see. I barely slept because I had so much to work on. Sometimes, I worried it would never work out.

(Spoiler alert: it worked out!)

I'm so grateful my parents relented and let me follow the career path I wanted. I've learned that the more you enjoy what you do, the easier it is to be successful in it, because you truly want to put everything into it that you can. The Aunties may be insulting about your artistic job because it's not the kind of 'classic' career they believe is sufficiently respectable. But just you watch – when they want free cosmetic products, makeup advice or a quick touch-up at a wedding, they'll suddenly be singing quite a different tune about the worthiness of your talents!

You'll find the same goes for any creative job. They'll

roll their eyes about your fashion design course, then slyly ask if you'd be willing to make them a new sari. Or they'll loudly wonder why on earth you decided to become a gourmet chef, before casually assuming you'll cater their next party for free.

I'm truly thankful for the sacrifices our elders made. Many of them didn't have the choice to become a musician, or volunteer for a local charity, because doing so would have meant they didn't eat. And maybe a lot of potential enjoyment and fulfilment for them was lost as a result.

But I believe those sacrifices were for a reason: to open up a freer life, with more choice, for their families' future generations. So why should we repeat the same patterns now? Because of our elders' hard work, some of us now have the chance to pursue a career doing what we love, because we already have a roof over our heads and food on the table. We can do what truly makes us happy.

I know that I was very lucky – not everyone has parents who'll give in. Some young brown people will get threatened with alienation or eviction if they choose to follow a different career path to the one their family favours. And, of course, not all of us have families who are financially able to support us, even if they do encourage our dreams.

If you find yourself suddenly needing an income to support yourself, and fast, that massively limits your ability to go for unpaid or low-paid work. Some of us really do need to make sure we make ends meet, for ourselves and perhaps also to support others.

But we're no longer in a world where the arts are shunned and frowned upon. There are more jobs in creative industries than ever before. Plus, what's the harm in getting some extra cash through a side hustle such as working as a barista, or in a pub, if it helps financially? You can still make money, even if it may take a while for your acting or singing or sculpting career to click.

I understand that it's not always so simple to make your dreams come true. Sometimes, we have other responsibilities that stop us from pursuing our passions for a while. Your family might really need financial support, with your income being vital to make sure everyone is fed and sheltered. Perhaps you've got to help run the family business to make ends meet. Some parents might dictate your career and fate to you, not giving you a lot of choice at all.

Most parents will want nothing but security for their children, and maybe orchestrating your career path gives them their own sense of security. It gives them great consolation knowing that they have chosen a profession for you that they believe will provide a secure future, that you won't have to go through the financial hardships they had to. But I can imagine how difficult it is, especially if you don't get the space to voice how you really feel. After all that, you just don't have the energy or mental capacity to try to explore your personal interests. It can be a bit depressing when you don't have the freedom to do anything but prioritise what you *need* to do over what you *want* to do.

Remind yourself that the situation is not for ever. Maybe right now, you need to put your own desires on hold. But they're not cancelled, they're not gone. They're on pause, and a time may well come when you *do* have the opportunity to explore them. The time will come when the family business is thriving without your help. The time will come when you feel ready to turn your focus to your dreams. You've proven your dedication to your family, and no one can doubt that they'll always be your top priority. But now it's your time.

When that time comes, my advice is to show your family how interested and talented you are in your chosen field. Find plenty of examples of people who've had success in the same area. Planning is key: explain to them your clear route and journey of how you'll progress and prosper. Your own enthusiasm and determination are your biggest assets – let your family see them shine.

Of course, in the brown community there are many women who choose not to have a professional career, pro-portionally more so than for white people. Many decide to focus on getting married when they're younger, while others give up their paid job when they become a wife or a mother.

If you're a housewife and mother, you know it's incred-ibly demanding and requires a lot of toil, and not just emotionally: raising the children, cooking the food, cleaning and washing, all manner of exhausting things to keep the household running smoothly. It's because of your support that your partner is even able to go out and be the bread-winner. If you know that being a homemaker is what you want to do, then your choice is just as valid and valuable as anyone else's. It doesn't matter if you're not directly on the payroll – you're still a boss!

There are so many options out there for pursuing what

you truly enjoy and care about, while still maintaining a healthy and joy-filled lifestyle. I don't believe any of us should force ourselves into a job we don't feel any excitement for if we don't have to.

Trust me, I know. It was only when I decided to pursue something I was genuinely invested in that I started on the road to happiness and success.

Brown Girl Problems

'*I have extended desi family who always want to see me fail, because they're jealous of me for performing better than their own kids.*'

Ah, yes. Beware the *nazar*.

If you fail in life, the Aunties will tell you that you need to do better. But if you succeed? The Aunties will tell you to be careful, because the *nazar*, or evil eye, is on you. In other words, if you do well, then there'll be someone jealously eyeing your achievement and wishing misfortune on you as a result. That someone could well be one of the Aunties themselves. So, watch out.

There's really just no way to win, is there?

Sadly, not only is there an unhealthy obsession with overachieving and securing a good job in the Asian community, there's also a massive, unspoken competition going on between families at all times. I say 'unspoken' in the sense that no one explicitly acknowledges the competition, but a lot of it *does* get fought through speech. For example:

'My daughter got all A*s in her exams. How did *you* do?'

'My son is a banker, and he just got an amazing Christmas bonus. Oh, do you not get a bonus in your line of work?'

'That's great that you got a new job. *My* daughter is happy where she is, and she's told she'll be getting a promotion next year.'

Honestly, if you succeed, then there's a good chance your parents and close family will be showing off about you like this. It's a bit cringe, to say the least. And the Aunties will *not* like it, because it'll make them feel inferior.

Whereas if you fail, then it gives the Aunties so much more to be smug about.

It's not only the Aunties that want to see you fail; some of their children do, too. They've had the 'must be the best' mantra hammered into their heads all their lives. And they believe you can't be the best unless everyone else falls short.

In their minds, you are their enemy, and they need to get one up on you. It doesn't matter if you're studying a subject that has nothing to do with their own academic career in any way, they'll still find ways to compare. 'Oh, you got an A in drama? Well, *I* got a B in chemistry, and everyone *knows* that chemistry is *much harder.*' Honestly, cuz, with that kind of theatrical reaction, I think you could get an A in drama too.

It's even worse if you end up studying the same subject or trying to get into the same industry. Prepare for every step you take to be scrutinised and analysed and judged, because it's ever so important for your cousin to know that they're doing better than you.

It can be a competitive environment; they want to be better than you, either by actually *being* better than you or, if that doesn't work, wishing you are worse off than them. So they'll congratulate your recent success through gritted teeth, and hope you'll never see its like again.

Look, I'm not saying this is what all brown people are like – of course it's not. But the side effect of a culture which places so much value on stable careers and financial success is that sometimes people take it way too seriously. They measure themselves, and everyone else, by these goals of academic achievement, career progression and wealth. They'll even turn their own relatives into rivals.

It sounds like this is what's happened to you. So what to do about it?

Well, it may sound easier said than done, but first of all, bask in your own achievements. The ill-will and envy of others does not at all change what you've accomplished. You've worked hard and you have skills and talent; you deserve everything you attain for yourself.

Humility is also very important. You could and should be proud of what you do, but there's also no need to rub it in other people's faces. Not that I think you're doing that! I know most of us brown girls actually tend to be quite shy about the wonderful things we achieve, and if anything we should be more confident about how awesome we are.

I do think, though, that our parents do need to try to tone down the bragging a little. It's wonderful that they're so proud, but maybe they don't have to start *every* family conversation with their child's latest accomplishment. I think it just starts a vicious cycle. One parent shows off about their child, so the other gets jealous and shows off about theirs, so the *other* gets jealous . . .

If you know your parents are the sort to gush a little bit *too* much about your successes, maybe have a little chat with them about the importance of modesty, alongside pride. They can be forgiven for wanting to shout from the rooftops about their little girl's latest success, but there's a time and place. Hopefully that will reduce your extended family's less than celebratory reactions.

Perhaps, though, your parents are already the unassuming, understated sorts. I bet they're overflowing with pride about you, but it could be that they're outwardly humble, and don't stoke the competition at all. If it's all just coming from your extended family, then what can you do?

I'm sorry to say, but some people are just bitter. They cannot stop focusing on what others have and think about very little else. If your extended family members keep wishing for you to crash and burn, despite the best efforts of you and your family to not brag about, or even downplay, your achievements, the best advice I can give is: forget about them.

Focus on your goals and your life. You know it's not a competition, so why act like it is? Your accomplishments are your own, and have nothing to do with anyone else.

If there are people out there crossing their fingers for you to fail, you'll wind up proving them wrong. It'll feel amazing. But it'll feel even better because you didn't devote all your time and energy just to spite them.

They may have an evil eye on you, but you just keep your eyes on the prize.

'I desperately want to go into fashion design, but I live with my parents, and they refuse to let me drop out of my dentistry course even though they know I'm close to failing it.'

When you live with your parents, it's a lot tougher to conceal what you're doing. Sure, you could drop out of your dentistry course and just not tell them, but they'd pretty quickly wonder why your lecture times have changed; why your classmates coming round for group project work are totally different people to before; why your orthodontic textbooks seem to have been replaced with dyes and pattern papers.

If an official-looking letter arrives with your name on it, your parents might casually tear it open, assuming you have nothing to hide. And when it's an enrolment certificate for your exciting new fashion design course, then they're not exactly going to be thrilled.

Lying is rarely the best course of action in any scenario, even if you don't think you'll get found out. For something like this, which affects your entire life and future, trust me: you *will* get found out. And the deceit will hurt everyone.

What can you do instead?

I can't sympathise enough with how horrible it is, forcing

yourself through studies that you have no interest or enjoyment in. Your classmates seem to be doing fine, and fair play to them if this is what they have a passion for. But you? You're struggling to achieve the marks you need to, not at all because you're stupid or slow, but because deep down it all just feels so pointless. Getting good marks would just move you further along towards a goal you don't even want to achieve.

Your mind wanders off to fashion trends and catwalk ideas, so it's even harder to focus on tooth decay and gum disease. You're stretching yourself thin, striving to make your brain process knowledge it just isn't interested in retaining. You try to look ahead to the future, but all you see is yourself battling with this kind of misery every single day. When your own parents don't seem to care about your distress, it can feel a lot like you have nowhere to go.

I think it's important to understand why your parents are so keen on your dentistry course. I can hazard a guess. You don't often hear about chronically unemployed dentists, do you? It's all about them making sure you have a solid, reliable career. They want to be certain you'll never want for money.

But that's not the whole story. We need to analyse deeper. Why, exactly, is it so important to your parents that you have a stable income?

Well, it's because they want to know you'll be able to support yourself. They want to know you can get yourself food, shelter, nice things. They want to know that, when they're gone, you'll still have a good life.

The absolute foundation of it is: your parents want you to be happy.

Yeah. It *really* doesn't feel that way, does it?

I believe the best way forward with your parents is to encourage them to drill down into what it is they really want for you, which is almost certainly your happiness. Then explain to them that, while having a stable income definitely brings some relief, it's not the only crucial component in a person's life.

Explain that you're close to failing because you're miserable. Explain that trying to do this work every day for the rest of your life will only make you more miserable. Explain that money and possessions could never make up for that constant, churning unhappiness and anxiety in your stomach.

Explain that, although they're seeking your happiness, forcing you to pursue a career you just don't want to do will actually achieve the exact opposite of what they want. Explain that true happiness is simply not something that can be bought.

I appreciate this will not necessarily be an easy conversation. But it will be an honest one. It's my hope that, after some self-reflection, your parents will finally understand.

'I want to start a YouTube channel, but OnlyFans pays more and quicker.'

First of all, for those readers who don't know what OnlyFans is, I'm going to give you a moment to Google

GET A PROPER JOB'

it quickly – that is, of course, if you're eighteen or over. I cannot be held responsible for anything you see. Still, I apologise in advance.

Is everyone up to speed? Basically, OnlyFans is an app where users can create content for their fans, who pay a subscription for access. That content could, theoretically, be anything. In general, though, it's explicit – nude photos, sexy videos and other amateur pornographic material.

Yeah, you get the gist now. Okay, let's continue.

Sis, let me just tell you now: if anyone sees or finds out, you *won't* be getting a round of applause from your family. If you're going to go down the OnlyFans road, then the only clapping you'll see is from someone's booty cheeks. Not quite my thing, but that is totally up to you!

Now, I am all for doing what you want and doing what makes you happy. And I also try my best not to jump to conclusions. Who knows how you're planning to use the platform? OnlyFans is used for a ton of different purposes. You could be creating makeup tutorials on there, or sharing music you've made, or asking for people's opinions on the clothes you've designed.

Or, you could be making it clap for some quick dollar dollar.

If we're going with the latter, I want to be completely real with you and not sugar-coat the truth. Because I think you already know it.

Every single Auntie you know, along with your By-the-Book and possibly even On-The-Fence and Wild West brown girls, are most certainly going to have something to say about your OnlyFans. And it's highly unlikely to be positive.

You'll probably get called all sorts of names, and if you don't hear any of them, it'll sadly be because they're being thrown at you behind your back. Your OnlyFans content won't just stay on OnlyFans – you'll have all sorts of screen-shots sent around to your mum, your dad, your brother ... urgh. And you'll definitely be a hot topic when you turn up to family occasions. Some might not be shy of giving you a blatant a dirty look or two. Oh, you'll still see some smiling faces, though, because those distant and so-called Uncles certainly won't hesitate to approach you, and that's probably not the attention you're looking for.

As we know, brown girls sexualising themselves is a big no-no in any context. Dressing up in revealing clothes, just because we like it, is forbidden. So there's no chance in hell that anyone will think it's acceptable for you to make money through your body. I think, brown or not, most communities would be a little shocked. Imagine a little old Auntie is tuning into your channel to watch you share whatever it is you're doing: art, singing, dancing. Then the next clip on autoplay is pornographic. If it's you, well, that Auntie will probably have an actual heart attack, and people will spend the entire funeral telling you it's your fault. And if it's not you, it still doesn't exactly come across as a good look.

I believe, wholeheartedly, that whatever you choose to do should make you feel good in some way, and be empower-ing. At the same time, I personally think it's very important to think about your future and how you're seen by the world, in addition to how you see yourself. I wouldn't want my spontaneous actions of today to creep back up on me later down the line and affect me negatively.

OK, let's assume that it's not your plan to post explicit content and that you're looking for an easy-to-use channel to post daily vlogs, DIY hacks or maybe you're an excellent cook and want to share your delicious recipes with the world. If you've also considered YouTube and think it's too hard, then I can say with authority that, yes, YouTube *is* hard. But so is any job that's worth having. The reward is always so much sweeter when you know you worked hard for it. YouTube is also great for reaching wider audiences.

On the other hand, if you enjoy OnlyFans as a platform because you feel there's an endless amount of talent on there (and I'm not speaking about sexual talents) and you want to be a part of it, then go for it. You never know when and where your career might take you and you'll get noticed for the content you're creating. As a creative, you don't want to pigeonhole yourself into one platform, anyway. Only you know where you feel you might attract the type of audience you're looking for, and maybe OnlyFans is the place where you find people that you can relate to.

As tempting as OnlyFans is, as well as any other platform giving you quick and easy money for doing very little, there's a reason it's like that. I personally think it's not worth it. The quick money I made now might be great, but I wouldn't want to regret it in a few years' time when the pictures have been leaked to my younger cousin's school, or been found by my potential employers who decide not to hire me after all. And let alone what other people thought, I don't think I'd feel right in myself; I'd always feel I'd crossed a personal line and could never go back. At the end of the day, I just don't believe quick money is ever worth compromising my morals over.

Yes, I know, I sound like a prude. I promise I'm a pretty chilled person about most things. I'm outspoken, and I love to break the rules. But when it comes to porn and sex work, I'm about as By-the-Book as you can get. I sincerely think my body is a temple, and I wouldn't feel comfortable turning it into a commodity to make money from.

But let me be clear: that's just me.

I know there are a ton of brown girls out there, many of whom think and feel differently about this kind of thing. I've always thought one of the most beautiful parts of our world is its diversity of people, and that includes in beliefs like this.

Sis, if you genuinely want to get an OnlyFans, then go for it. I would just ask that you've taken into account the likely backlash you'll get from your local brown community. Not to mention, remember that once your content is on the internet, it's impossible to remove it completely. Don't believe anyone who tells you otherwise. Once it's out, it's out, and you never know where else it could end up. If you're okay to weather that storm, then credit where credit's due – you're a stronger woman than I am. As long as you've thought it through, and know in your heart of hearts that you'll have no regrets. Oh, and as long as you're an adult of course!

I'm afraid you won't be seeing me on OnlyFans any time soon, though. It's just not a way I can personally feel comfortable making money. For me, the road that leads to victory is always long and hard … excuse the pun.

'Why is it that when you're brown, everyone expects you to be smart? I'm not that good at school, and I'm not even sure if I want to go to uni.'

Being optimistic here, I think it's not the *worst* stereotype to have as a brown person. Right? Imagine if we were stereotyped for being the stupidest people on the planet. I know which one I'd pick!

But, look, I get it. Being stereotyped at all is incredibly annoying. People making pre-judgements solely based on your skin colour isn't nice. And the worst effect of all is it puts a whole load of pressure on you to live up to being someone that you're not.

Someone different. *Not* someone better.

I've felt the exact same as you before, especially when I've compared myself to my academically impressive brother, or heard about cousins passing their exams with flying colours. Meanwhile, I struggled a lot, and was happy to just pass at all!

I always thought that going to university was the normal and done thing to do. It's almost something you *have* to do if you want to be successful. It's such a standard part of chat for people in their twenties: 'Which uni did you go to?' There's an automatic assumption that we all did. Hence why I did a degree in special effects makeup.

If I think back: did I need to spend three years of my life doing this? Honestly, probably not. I would've been fine shadowing makeup artists, teaching myself practically, and altogether just being more hands-on. But because I'd watched every single person older than me go to university, I thought I had to do the same.

I'm not dissing anyone who went and enjoyed it. It's a great achievement, and any graduate should be proud of the hard work they put in to earn their degree. In addition, uni can also be a really fun experience where you learn so much about yourself and make amazing lifelong friends. There is loads to love.

On the other hand, it can genuinely also be a complete waste of time and money, especially for a lot of the more vocational and practical professions. It can cause loads of stress and panic over looming deadlines. Yes, university is the perfect fit for some people, and that's great. But it's not for everyone.

I suspect a lot of brown people go to university and get a degree purely so their parents can tell everyone that their children did it. They wear it like a badge of honour. What many brown families don't seem to understand is that there is absolutely no point in doing a degree for the sake of it. Finishing projects and doing exams can cause a real strain on mental health, especially when you know none of it may help you in future. And you might end up in a pool of debt for the privilege.

Your parents want to feel proud of you and want to see

you be successful. That's always their number-one priority. I sincerely think that many parents just don't know any better. Brown people believe school and a degree are the only path to happiness, but that's simply not true. You need to show them what other options there are, communicate with them, and constructively help them to understand better how you feel and what other options are available to you.

They're so focused on your education, but what about the ways you can educate them? This is the opportunity for you to teach them that academia is not the only way. Teach them that someone who's good at school isn't automatically better than everyone else. Teach them that you're worth so much more than the number or grade a teacher writes on a piece of paper. There are so many alternative routes, such as apprenticeships, short courses, or simply contacting the right people to get hands-on experience. Yes, you may hear a fair few 'no's' in the process, but eventually you'll receive a 'yes' from someone, and that someone could be your gateway to an amazing career. No exams required.

You may not be that good at school, which I understand can be quite confidence-crushing. I've been there. However, there are other things that you're good at. Maybe even the best at. Whether you know what that is now, or if you're going to find it out about yourself later down the line, there is always something. I promise. Keep the faith and remember: there's a lot more to life than school.

Brown Girl Wisdom

Nothing in life really worth having is easy. But if you truly enjoy what you do, then you'll want to put that extra effort and time in. As a result, that hard work becomes a lot less hard to do. On the other hand, if you're trying to make yourself follow a career that your heart isn't in, then that hard work becomes even harder. So follow your passion.

Because creative activities shouldn't just be seen as hobbies. Makeup, art, acting, fashion, music, dance, writing, photography, you name it – they all take enormous skill and dedication. No less so than following a more traditional profession.

Think of all these wonderful South Asian women who defied the trend, making their way in artistic and creative fields:

- Anamika Khanna, whose fusion of Indian and Western styles has earned her features in *Vogue* and a reputation as one of the top Indian fashion designers.
- Raja Kumari, an award-winning rapper and songwriter who's worked with such famous figures as Gwen Stefani and Iggy Azalea, and is set to become just as big a name.
- Manal Mirza, a Muslim-American-Pakistani designer and illustrator who's been acclaimed for her striking, relatable artwork.
- Shilpa Ray, a singer-songwriter whose captivating

indie-blues style has led her to collaborations with the likes of Patti Smith and Nick Cave.

• Aishwarya Sridhar, who at twenty-three in 2020 became the first and youngest Indian woman adult to win a category in the Wildlife Photographer of the Year Awards.

They've all proven that a brown woman can be successful and influential in fields that were once considered out of bounds.

But, hey, if you're not so artistically inclined, then don't feel like you have to be. It's my bag, sure, but that doesn't mean it's everyone's. Absolutely follow your interest in science, or business, or healthcare, or sport. You can have passion in anything; it doesn't have to be something outwardly splashy and colourful. Only you know how you feel about it, and how much it excites you to learn more. If you've found the thing you want to learn, grow and work in, then go for it.

And if you haven't?

It's not just the brown community. The subjects we all study at school, college or university are decided when we are still quite young, and are meant to set the course for what we do in the future. I think it's incredibly unfair. We're still discovering ourselves in our teens and early twenties; it's impossible to know with certainty exactly what we want to do.

Look at me. I tried nursing because it seemed a 'good' subject to do. And it is, for so many wonderful people, for whom I have nothing but the utmost respect. But it didn't quite fit me. I didn't feel that spark. Then, out of the blue, I had a revelation about what I genuinely *wanted* to do. And a YouTube career was born!

Of course, it's easy for me to sit here and talk about my flash of inspiration. All very well and good, Anchal. But what about those of you who haven't been sent a sign?

I say, go for what suits you in the moment, right now.

It's important to make an effort in every subject in school, whether you're academically inclined or not. It allows you to keep your options open later down the line. When it comes to choosing which GCSEs or A Levels to study, you'll have already discovered which subjects you enjoy putting the work into, and which ones you don't feel so excited about. You'll have the experience to choose the subjects that you're genuinely interested in, rather than just opting for what seems good on paper or what other people want you to do.

If university doesn't appeal to you, don't go. Check out opportunities for local work or volunteering, and see if there's anything you find you'd be happy doing day after day. Explore career options online, and talk to the people around you who seem happy and fulfilled in their professions. It takes effort, research and trying out new things, but you will eventually find the thing that clicks. Focus on what you enjoy spending your time on, rather than what seems like it'll get you paid.

Perhaps you've already established a career, but you've realised that your chosen path isn't quite giving you that spark. Maybe you know you'd be happier doing something else. It could be that the law degree you decided to do when you were eighteen isn't fulfilling you any more and you're interested in learning about how to become a nutritionist. Or the sales job where you spend hours working to someone else's deadlines and targets, which you were initially excited about, now feels like a mundane chore, and you would much rather be building your own brand. My advice would be to spend a couple of hours every week, or more if you can afford to, researching a new career. Find out what kinds of roles are available. Check if there are opportunities to retrain or study a course in the field. Reach out to people at companies you'd be interested in working at, and ask for advice. If what you discover feels appealing, you'll know to keep pursuing it – and if not, you'll be armed with more information to explore alternative options. I honestly believe it sometimes just takes a little nudge in a different direction, and all of a sudden you'll find a fire in your belly.

Most of all, remember that people's careers grow and change all the time. You should never feel you're locking yourself into one box for ever, with all other options closed off.

Now, for some, having a career may not appeal at all. Especially for some By-the-Book brown women who may want to focus on motherhood, as is traditional. I don't judge whatsoever. If you don't want a paid career, then don't have one. You're certainly working more than hard enough as a homemaker, anyway. The amount of effort and skill required is sometimes undervalued, but it shouldn't be, because the work you do is vital and appreciated.

My advice is: you never know what the future holds. People with happy, secure marriages sometimes find their lives unexpectedly torn apart for a number of different reasons, whether it be because of infidelity, or an accident, or an illness. I hope and pray none of this misfortune happens to any of us, but sometimes life has other ideas. Suddenly, you may find yourself alone, with children to feed and no income.

Money is important. I'll never pretend it's not. We all need to be able to look after ourselves and any loved ones who depend on us, by making sure we have a safe shelter and food to eat. It's okay to want some perks, like new makeup or nice clothes or the odd holiday. These experiences are a part of living life to the fullest, and, yes, they require money. We don't all have a family who is able to provide that kind of support. So, if we're able to, we need to try to do it for ourselves.

Perhaps it won't be the most inspiring work in the world at first – getting food on the table is the biggest priority, after all. If your circumstances have changed abruptly, income will probably take priority over personal fulfilment. But even if you're unable to follow your passions right now, you're still a worthwhile, talented person, and you can learn to be good at whatever you need to do. So if the time comes when you find you unexpectedly need to make money to survive, believe in yourself that you can do it. Because you can. We all can.

What we need often trumps what we want – that's the way life goes. But I still believe it's important to be honest about what we want to do. Even if you don't currently have the freedom to do what you want, try not to lose sight of your dreams. Spend an hour here and there looking into how you can pursue them, when the time is right.

It's a cliché, but doing what you enjoy and really care about is the best way to make money, and to make you happy.

So, now your career's sorted, it's time to find you a man!

Oh, you didn't think you could just be a strong and independent woman for ever, did you?

8

'I KNOW A LOVELY YOUNG BOY'

They always do. Every Auntie always knows a lovely young boy from a good family. How?! And why do they all happen to be dentists or doctors? Are all the dentists and doctors in the world just unable to find someone? Are they all listed in some kind of catalogue that the Aunties subscribe to? You'll never hear an Auntie say, 'I know a lovely young boy from a good family. He's a music producer.' They'll only ever tell you about the 'professional' ones – or, at least, the 'professional' ones are the only guys the Aunties would ever call 'lovely young boys'.

Okay. Rant over.

I'll start from the beginning.

When you're younger, dating isn't even a concept. It's completely off limits. Screw that, actually – even *talking* to the opposite sex, in any context or for any reason at all, is completely off limits. Well, it was for me at least. My parents sent my sisters and me to an all-girls school, and you can guess where my brother went – yep, an all-boys school.

This is a quick but important message to all parents out there who are considering sending their child to a same-sex school purely because they want their child to only focus on education throughout school, and not get distracted. *It doesn't work.* They will still, at some point, despite all your very best efforts, get distracted. If anything, making the opposite sex seem so elusive and off limits might make your child even *more* likely to get distracted.

Let me explain.

Where I went to school, there was a boys' school nearby; for some events and performances, the schools would collaborate. This included the annual Valentine's disco (which I wasn't allowed to go to until Year 9, and even then I had to *beg* my parents to let me attend!). It was every girl's one chance to make an impression, and for the guys to show off their best swagger. And with both schools being same-sex, everyone was pretty much permanently thirsty, or at the very least craved some attention.

It was a pure embarrassment – every single year. The girls weren't used to speaking to boys, the boys weren't used to speaking to girls, and no one was used to pretending *so hard* that we were casual and confident, when we felt anything but. Every girl trying to be a woman, every boy trying to be a man, and the result being a room full of sweaty nervous teenagers stuttering over their words and stumbling over their feet. Not the sexy, sophisticated affair any of us were hoping for.

The schools also used to come together for the big school play every year. I loved drama in school (naturally) and one year, at about fourteen or fifteen years old, I auditioned for a part. I got a decent role – basically, I wasn't an extra and had a fair number of lines, but for me, being the small Indian girl that definitely didn't think of herself as the most attractive (and wasn't even allowed to do her eyebrows or upper lip yet), this was an achievement!

We got the scripts, and I went to a couple of the script run-throughs before proper rehearsals – which, by the way, all took place in the strange foreign land that was *the boys' school*. This was all so new and exhilarating for me.

As the teacher read through the script with us, it suddenly became clear: there was a scene in the play where my character would kiss one of the boys.

I played it cool, at that moment in time, and just nodded along. No problem. All good. Super chill.

The whole walk home, however, I freaked out.

What was I going to do?! All I could think was:

I don't fancy this boy

I'VE NEVER KISSED ANYONE

OMG MY PARENTS ARE GOING TO WATCH THE PLAY AND SEE ME KISS A BOY

Hell. No.

I quit. I never went back. If simply talking to boys was off limits, I sure as anything wouldn't be allowed to kiss one, even if it was for a school play! I could just picture my parents, shame painting horrified frowns on their faces, as I imagined it.

I mean, I'd never even kissed a boy at all. For the sake of the play, I might have gathered together my courage, thrown myself into character and just gotten on with it . . . except I didn't *particularly* want my first kiss to be under my parents' appalled gaze. Hardly the kind of thing you dreamily write in your diary about!

If I tried to go through with it, I knew I'd be terrified the entire time. I wouldn't be able to concentrate on my performance. I'd be worrying and worrying and worrying. What if my dad decided to be embarrassing and pull me out of the play *mid-show*?! And he would. I knew he would. Then I'd be known in school as 'the girl whose dad pulled her out of the school play'. Absolutely not the persona I wanted to craft for myself.

I couldn't face dealing with that humiliation. Leaving the play seemed like a far better idea. Sure, I'd miss out on the fun of acting – but no way, no *way*, was it worth all the anxiety.

That's the world a brown girl grows up in; as a child and a teenager, you're told that boys are essentially disgusting aliens who should be avoided at all costs. Even slightly associating with them could only bring danger, and shame. The result is that boys invade your mind, all the time, because you know there's way more to the story than you're being told. You want to find out more about them – they *look* human, but what strange secrets must they be keeping, in order to be so taboo? They seem so nearby, and yet forever out of reach. The further away you are from them, the more captivated you become.

Then, suddenly, as you enter adulthood in your late teens and early twenties, something switches. Suddenly, dating isn't only allowed, it's actively *encouraged*. You're not supposed to *avoid* the boys any more; now you're supposed to pick one to spend the entirety of the rest of your life with. And you're supposed to pick him *soon*. Now, all the Aunties are telling you about the 'lovely young boys' you should meet up with and get to know. Apparently, *girls* cannot date, but women can, should and *must*.

Of course, dating isn't really *dating* in South Asian culture. It's more like interviewing someone to marry. Guess what the name of the most popular Indian matchmaking service is? Shaadi.com – *shaadi* being the Hindi and Urdu word for wedding or marriage. Pretty upfront about the long-term commitment, isn't it? Definitely not like your casual Tinder hook-ups or chance Hinge meet-ups. Those apps aren't used so much in the brown community, especially not in the more By-the-Book circles. Instead, brown girls tend to stick to dating apps specifically for South Asian communities, like Dil Mil or Aisle, which focus on long-term commitments rather than quick flings. If the apps don't do it for them, then it's time to turn to a full-service operation like Shaadi.com, or a solo professional, such as Sima Taparia, who was featured on Netflix's *Indian Matchmaking*.

Or, of course, it's your local Auntie taking on the job full-time. Because marriage is a serious business.

And so, in true cutthroat business style, you're not

given much space for watching or waiting. Most of the time, you should know exactly what you want and who you're looking for.

Your family will have made it all pretty clear for you. There are unwritten rules about it all. We just know them, and are supposed to follow them. No one ever questions where they came from or whether we should change them; they simply *are*.

You have to find someone who has the same background as you; has a good job; and comes from a 'good family' (in other words, certain standards of class and wealth).

In a way, it's fairly simple and straightforward. Seeing as you know exactly what to look for, you obviously don't need to go on tons of dead-end dates, right? It's like going through a checklist, and once you've ticked everything off, that's it: perfect match, summer wedding, happy ever after. Sorted. After all, we all know (or, at least, the Aunties like to remind us) that being too fussy isn't good, either. So find someone who ticks the boxes and settle down. You're done.

Hmm ...

You see, I don't think dating is a means to an end. Dating is an experience, in and of itself. If you have a chance to just date, with no pressures or worries about getting married, there's so much fun and excitement to be had. You can relax and get to know someone more naturally. You can have an encounter that's a horrible, awkward disaster, and it doesn't have to feel like a fail-ure – it's just a hilarious story to add to your collection. Even the rejections, or the ones who didn't show up for date number two. It all just shapes you into a stronger person, someone that learns what they will and won't tolerate. You discover so much about yourself from going on all the good and bad dates.

I would love to say that every guy I've been out with has wined and dined me and showered me with expensive gifts, but I can't, because I would be lying to you. I once went on a date with a guy that kept whacking my arm and leg really hard every time he laughed. I wasn't sure if it was an excuse to touch me, or if he was naturally an aggressively touchy-feely kind of person, but it sure was annoying. Plus, it actually hurt!

I've also been on a couple of dates where all they've done, from start to finish, is speak about their ex, or their past relationships in general. If you're dating right now, let me tell you, that is a *big* no-no! It's the kind of thing that makes you want to say, 'I'm sorry, but I got a phone call when I went to the bathroom – there's an emergency and I have to leave right now!' Fingers crossed they're too polite to ask for details!

I think one of the worst times was where I ended up meeting this guy, going on a few dates, and to my surprise I saw potential for the future. We got on well and, more than that, I was mentally going through the tick boxes. Indian – *check*. Good job – *check*. Good family – *check*. Bingo.

Then, three months later, I found out he had been in a relationship with a girl for the past six years – a girl he knew he couldn't marry because of religious reasons. I was the side dish, in other words. Great!

They've not all been bad, though. I've had a few times where I've been on a date, literally *one* date with someone, and it's been an amazing night. The kind where you chat a bit, enjoy a few drinks and a good laugh, but you go home knowing nothing is going to come of it. That all-important 'spark' wasn't quite there. But you had a great night out, and isn't life about all the great nights out? It's a brilliant way of making friends as well – maybe you're not soul-mates, but you can still build a relationship together, even if it's a platonic one.

You see, without all these experiences, I wouldn't have a clue what I like or want in a potential partner. It's through all the dates – the good and the bad, the exciting and the dull, the ones that lasted for months and the ones that fizzled within half an hour – that I've come to know what I'm looking for. Learning about someone else's life, it's pretty cool – and it shines a light on what might make you happy one day.

I don't think the Aunties understand this idea at all. If a young woman is casually dating, the Aunties assume the worst (i.e. one night stands – the horror!). I'll talk more about this later, but most Aunties are fervently against sex before marriage. Obviously, for many people these days, premarital sex is a must in a relationship – it's a way to get to know their partner intimately, and to build a stronger connection. But the Aunties have no understanding that, in the right circumstances, it can be a healthy, dare I say helpful, thing.

Even without considering sex, they don't understand the idea of two people just getting to know each other,

without an assumption that wedding plans will be final-
ised by the end of date three.

So, what can we do?

Brown Girl Problems

**'How do you hide a relationship from brown
parents?'**

I'm actually quite shocked by this question. Not because
I think it's something a brown girl would never do – it's
actually because hiding relationships from our parents is
second nature to us brown girls. It's in our blood. We know
exactly what we're doing, and how not to get caught.

But if I must tell you, take note.

Let's start with the basics. First of all: *keep it off Instagram*.
You might think social media is a world your parents
will never know, but that's a huge mistake. If it isn't one of
your tech-savvy Aunties finding out (the Mild Aunties *love*
a good chain message on the family WhatsApp thread), it
will be a cousin you can't trust, and believe me, we all have
one of those. There will always be a way for it to get back
to your parents. Finding out through social media posts is
even worse than telling them yourself – first of all, there's
undeniable photographic evidence, and secondly, you'll be
accused of 'flaunting' your shame. There's no way of getting out of it. So don't do it – keep it off the feed.

Secondly, if you are at home or at family events, try not to be constantly hunched over your phone texting bae. It might sound innocent enough – you're just reading the news! You're just checking your email! – but it will seem suspicious. Brown families are nosy; they want to know *everything*. How's school? How's work? What did you do for your birthday? Why wasn't I invited? Do you have a boyfriend? Was your boyfriend invited to your birthday party?

And they'll have no shame in asking you why you're smiling at your phone too, most probably in front of a room full of people. It could genuinely just be a funny meme you've scrolled past on Twitter, but the Aunties will insist on being shown it. Even a Hot Auntie, who wants nothing to do with modern technology, will *demand* to know what's making you smile so much in public. I know I've been busted a couple of times for grinning at my phone, and it's so obvious when you're lying. Unless, of course, you're a good liar – but the Aunties are hard to fool for too long.

Trying to be on video calls or phone calls can be extremely difficult, and could give it all away to your parents if you're caught. Doesn't matter if your bedroom is on the opposite side of the house, one of your parents or siblings or Aunties will magically overhear every word. 'I was just coming up to collect your laundry for the wash,' your mum will say, 'and I heard you talking to someone – who is this boy?!'

We all know the key to successful phone calls is mastering the art of whispering. It's a delicate skill – you need to pitch it quietly enough that your family doesn't hear, but not so quiet that who you're talking to can't hear you either. If you can do this, you'll get by just fine.

Be aware, though, that your sleep pattern will probably be disturbed – longer phone calls can only happen at night when your parents are sleeping.

I want to be clear that I genuinely don't encourage lying to your parents, for a number of reasons. You love each other, and you don't want to cause a dent in that relationship; broken trust is hard to mend. However, for brown girls, because of all the many, many, *many* limitations and rules (no talking to boys, no staying out late, no drinking alcohol . . .), it just has to be done sometimes. It's the only way to have some freedom and to feel a little normal, a little more like everyone else, without potentially severing your relationship with your parents for good.

When you're telling your parents you're somewhere, but actually you're somewhere *else*, be sure to let at least one person know where you really are, for your own safety. This could be your girlfriend or a trusted sibling. And if you are breaking or bending the rules, don't take it too far. Make sure you come home at a somewhat reasonable hour. If your family calls, pick up. It'll make you feel better, and them. Besides, you want to do the absolute minimum to raise eyebrows and cause the Aunties to sniff around asking questions.

And this, right here, is me confessing that I've done all of the above. Sorry, Mum.

'I went on holiday with my man three times, but I feel bad that I did it without my parents knowing.'

A part of me wants to give you a round of applause for your bravery – not just once, but *three* times! The other part of me feels unbelievably stressed out on your behalf. I can't help but think, 'God forbid something happened to you and you're not even nearby for your family or parents to be there with you.'

This just reinforces my point – in general, brown girls know exactly how to hide relationships from their parents. They can even go on multiple holidays with their partner and keep it hidden. They'll do all the associated hard work around it, including not taking a single photo of the holiday, so it can't be tracked. These are the extreme lengths to which we will go, simply to enjoy what most Western people would consider totally standard things in a relationship.

You could be engaged, working a good job and paying your own way, and brown families will still have a problem with you going on holiday with your boyfriend. It should be a perfectly normal thing, and yet it's a huge source of controversy. I don't know why our parents and extended family members don't understand: when you're dating someone, and you like them or are even in love with them, you want to experience things together. And what better experience is there than jetting off somewhere nice and doing something completely new together? Who wouldn't want to explore the many varied and wonderful places in the world with someone they love spending time with?

For incomprehensible reasons known only to our parents and the Aunties, this is simply something that is only acceptable after you get married (along with so many other things).

Of course, there are alternatives. There are loads of stay-cations that you can do, and endless dinners out, and plenty of movies to see in the cinema. But then, what else? Yes, you like each other, and you'll be happy whatever you're doing – but wouldn't it be lovely to go somewhere *besides* the pub down the road, just for a change?

I also think that one of the best things about going on holiday with your partner, before you tie the knot, is that you can learn for sure whether or not you're able to spend day in, day out with each other. If your relationship can survive a holiday, it's one to hold on to. I believe this even when it comes to friendships.

I personally have never had the opportunity to go on holiday with a partner. I've always wanted to, but have been way too scared in case someone finds out. I have a big family, and if I'm lying to my parents, I'm either lying to all my siblings too, or I would have to get them involved in my lie and have them cover my tracks for any amount of days. I just couldn't do it to them.

Plus, my family is the type of family that sends each other pictures once we arrive somewhere – we even do little room video tours if it's somewhere special. How could I do that if I'm meant to be 'on a girls' holiday' or 'on a work trip'?

It would just get far too complicated, and I'm happy with my choice to avoid that whole scene. I am slightly jealous of those of you who've managed to pull it off safely and have that experience, though!

With regard to your experience, I say: what's done is done. You know your parents. You know how they'll react to things. You obviously didn't tell them you were going on holiday with your boyfriend for a reason. It's likely to be the same reason you might not want to come clean now. But what your parents don't know can't hurt them, and that's true whether you went on an illicit holiday once or three times.

However, the more you do it, the higher the risk becomes of someone finding out, or even of you being overwhelmed by guilt and telling them yourself. Whether you're planning to open up to them or not, be prepared for any consequences you may have to face if they do find out, most significantly that they'll probably lose trust in you. You know them best, and only you know how much more this will eat you up if you don't tell them. If the guilt does feel like it's getting too much, then come clean. At least that way, no matter what the consequences are, you know you have this off your chest and you can hopefully start with a clean slate. No more secret holidays.

But hey, I really admire that you're trying to do the things that make you happy. At the end of the day, it's your call.

'My parents think my best friend just likes to hang out at mine a lot. She's actually my girlfriend and I don't know how to tell them.'

If I were dating a girl, this is exactly what I would do too. You could get away with it for years and years, and no one would bat an eyelid.

Hey, I'm pretty sure my family probably think I might be a lesbian, considering I never mention any guys to them. I always go to my 'girlfriends' houses' in the evenings, and I spent all of my younger years pretending to be disgusted by boys so as not to raise eyebrows. Even now, as a mature and confident woman, I still won't mention them. Boys? Urgh, gross.

If keeping boys a secret is hard (and it really is), I can't imagine how you feel having to keep a same-sex relationship under wraps. Sure, what you're doing is working now, for the time being at least. But for how many more weeks, months, years can you keep it up? What happens when it's 'time to get married'?

Sooner or later, your family will start getting much more invested in who you're dating. You can't keep the ruse up for ever. And who would even *want* to keep it up for ever?

I can imagine the constant lying is very hard for you, and, in all honesty, it won't get any easier. Your girlfriend is probably regularly walking in, saying hello to your parents, sharing dinners and stories and laughs, building a bond – but all under a big pretence. That's tough – for you, for your parents, and for your girlfriend. What happens when the façade comes crashing down and they find out the truth?

And don't assume that they don't already have their suspicions. I always wonder, 'Do my parents know I'm lying?' Part of me always figures that they can just tell. Because, you know, they're my parents. They made me. They know my face and my gestures and the tone of my voice better than anyone else. Of *course* they know when I'm lying, no?

When we're hiding things, over time, our parents do sometimes realise what's going on. They can just feel it. But that doesn't mean they'll confront you with it. Very often, and especially in the case of a suspected same-sex attraction, they'll choose to bury their heads in a sand of deep denial.

I know that most brown families would never want to 'admit' that their son or daughter is gay, or bisexual, or gender non-conforming. If the Aunties catch you holding hands with someone of the same sex, it's game over! That's the absolute hottest tea for them, and it will be all over town in minutes. They will never, ever stop to consider your feelings or what you could be going through. Unfortunately, you basically have the choice of keeping your sexuality a totally hidden secret, or having it shared and judged by every single person you've ever met.

It's a real shame to have to say it, but a lot of the brown community still haven't accepted the LGBTQ+ community. To be LGBTQ+ if you're Asian is almost considered the same as having an extreme illness. Something about you, deep within you, is 'wrong' and 'broken': either your parents messed up raising you; or you were exposed to 'bad influences' at school; or you were allowed to watch too many makeover shows on TV – all of these crazy, wild, completely irrational excuses, simply to try to explain why you are who you are.

As a result, there's an awful and utterly unfair stigma associated with being LGBTQ+. If a son or daughter is brave enough to come out, unless their parents are extremely open-minded, they're unlikely to be greeted with love and congratulations. Instead, their parents will most probably be openly devastated. Above all else, they'll cry: *How will we face the community?*

And the nosy Auntie who lives next door will overhear the ensuing argument and smugly think: *That won't happen to* my *child. That won't happen to* my *family.*

And what if it does, Auntie? What if it does?

I know in my family it's been quite a struggle for some of the gay men. They've had to hide it all their lives, their parents making excuses as to why they're not in relationships and flatly ignoring what's happening right under their noses. And I can assure you: these are the sons of the *Hot* Aunties. Ironic, isn't it? The Hot Aunties incessantly gossip about everyone else around them, yet they don't notice what's happening in their own homes, or spare a moment to consider the wants and needs of their own children. And so those children live in fear, of being mentally and sometimes physically abused if they dare to speak up about who they really are.

As with practically everything else, there's a huge double

standard when it comes to this. It's something I've always been so confused by.

A few years back I went to a Kashmiri wedding, and a year or so later I attended a family wedding in Punjab. I noticed an interesting common trend on both occasions. At the weddings, they invite gay men, dressed as women, who come to perform, sing, dance and generally entertain for a short while. If you're picturing an Asian version of a stripper, you're pretty much spot on – people even give them money as they dance around the room. They're invited because they're seen as lucky; however, while they're appreciated for some entertainment, they're still outcast from general society. If this is what one of the Aunties' sons were doing, I can bet she wouldn't see it as lucky. She'd probably claim she never had a son at all.

The brown community still have a lot of work to do, and a long way to go, with regard to educating themselves on LGBTQ+ matters. We can barely talk about sexual orientation, and discussions around being transgender and gender identity are still a distant conversation unfortunately.

It's a frustrating place to be in, but I do have hope that we may one day be in a more compassionate, understanding environment with respect to homosexuality, bisexuality and gender non-conformity. There are some brilliant organisations out there doing wonderful work in this area. If you and your girlfriend ever need somewhere to turn, there's the Naz and Matt Foundation, which helps tackle homophobia triggered by religion in order to help parents accept their LGBTQ+ children. There's also the Gaysian

Organisation, a great network for South Asians with tons of ways to support you.

I have faith that one day, such understanding will be offered to all LGBTQ+ people a lot closer to home, meaning our brothers, our sisters, and our nearest and dearest will have to face less homophobia, biphobia and transphobia. Our brown community prizes family above all else, and it means there's so much love and affection there, even if it's not always shown. A gay child obviously deserves to receive the same amount of unconditional love as if they were straight. My hope is that a family's love for their child is stronger than their adherence to these narrow-minded, outdated prejudices.

As for your current situation with your girlfriend, my advice would be to speak to your family when you're ready.

How will you know you're ready, though?

Your gut. It will tell you, and you'll just know the time is now.

The worst thing would be for your parents to have to hear rumours from someone else. Certain people like to twist things, and deliberately make the story sound more salacious, so it justifies them gossiping about you. You don't need your parents hearing about how you were leading some kind of flamboyant gay pride march when, actually, it was just a non-eventful lunch with your girl-friend at Nando's.

It will always be better coming from you. And, yes, your parents might find it hard to accept. It could take them a while. But because *you* told them, and not a random Auntie or your bad vibes cousin, they'll be more inclined to have your back. Wouldn't you rather your parents responded to the informant with 'I already know' than 'Oh God, no'?

However, situations don't always pan out the way we hope they will. There are families who wouldn't blink an eye at kicking you out, or worse. I hope and pray your parents are supportive, but, unfortunately, that doesn't necessarily mean they will be.

It's best to mentally sketch out different scenarios of how you think telling your family will go, and prepare a plan of action for each one. Go from the best scenario to the worst, so you can think about how to handle each potential situation. Make sure you have at least one person, such as a trusted friend or a partner, who you can lean on in the event things don't go well. That includes sorting out offers of accommodation in the extreme case it turns out that you can't stay at home.

And certainly don't hesitate to contact support groups and charities, such as those I recommended earlier and are listed in the back of this book. They've seen and heard it all, and will know how to guide you if the worst comes to the worst. I can imagine you feel so isolated right now, but you're not alone. So many other people have been through the same thing. There will be people who love you and understand, no matter what happens.

It is my hope that, even while preparing for the worst, you find you are pleasantly surprised with a better outcome than you were anticipating. Things can sometimes work out beautifully. It's happened to LGBTQ+ brown girls before. Sometimes, their parents wind up being their biggest advocates and defenders. I hope the same is true for you.

But if it isn't, in all of this, don't lose sight of who you are or apologise for it. Regardless of what anyone may say, you're you, and you're perfect the way you are. You have nothing to be ashamed of.

You'll know when you can't keep the secret for any longer. Your girlfriend pretending to be 'just a friend' won't be fun any more and, if anything, it could harm your relationship. So, prepare yourself, make some plans, and follow your gut. Above all, reach out for support. Best of luck – I'm rooting for you.

'I don't like my brother's girlfriend, and they're getting more serious.'

For anyone who is not from a brown family, one thing you need to understand is that you are never just dating your partner – you're dating their whole family. Or, to be even more accurate, the whole family is dating you.

When you're dating someone from a brown family, it's so important that everyone likes you. It's a lot of pressure. I can't imagine how scary it must have been for my own brother's wife when she came to meet his siblings. Three sisters. Three *older* sisters. And I must say, not one of us is shy or quiet.

I understand how difficult it is to be in your position. You can't help it if you don't like someone; sometimes, two people just don't click, and that's the way it is. But at the same time, you don't want to dislike her so much that it causes a rift between you and your brother. No matter what your feelings about her are, you never want to lose that sibling connection. Family is everything.

It's important to try to understand the things that he likes about her. It sounds like you care about your brother and get on well with him, so it's unlikely he's fallen in love with someone who's completely irredeemable, right? Perhaps he enjoys her sense of humour, or maybe she's amazingly supportive when he's down. There's undeniably something about his girlfriend and their relationship that your brother's decided he wants to keep in his life for ever.

In Asian families, we sometimes tend to bypass someone's core happiness because it doesn't satisfy our own needs or meet our own standards. What you have to remember is that you're not the person dating her. You're not the one who has to have pillow talk with her, or take her out on dates. As long as this new girlfriend of your brother's isn't being nasty or manipulative, or you're noticing something really not quite right at all, then your brother's happiness is what matters most. If your brother is happy, then you have to find happiness in yourself for him.

Just imagine it being the other way around. Think about when you have liked someone, or want to do something and you've made your mind up about it. You might not have been 100 per cent certain about it, but you were keen to explore.

But then, along came Auntie who wants to rain on your parade a little. She noticed something unappealing about your idea. She decided you'd be happier if you did something or chose someone else.

It can put you off. You're left there, agonising about your decision and not knowing what to do. But Auntie? She's already forgotten about it and moved on. It's a matter that doesn't concern her. She most likely didn't even listen to you, or try to look at why you even wanted to explore that route. Yet, she was happy to put negative thoughts in your head, and then wander off. Remember, the decisions you make in your life are nothing to do with her.

You don't want to be Auntie in this situation. You don't want to live your brother's life for him.

Whatever you do should be your decision. And whatever your brother does should also be his decision.

You love your brother, and surely someone he's opened his heart to can't be all bad? Try to look for the things he sees, understand his point of view, and learn to like her.

It might be that you've tried that already, so if you've decided she really *is* bad news – for example because she's abusive or manipulative – and you can see that this relationship will harm or hurt your brother, then there's obviously no point sitting around attempting to make friends with her.

In this situation, try to talk to your brother about it. If you're actively worried about him, he needs to hear your perspective. However, when you do it, remove all your own personal feelings. This is not about you, or why you don't like her. You need to explain to him exactly what you've noticed about her that you believe is harmful, and the reasons you're concerned for his well-being. Speak in a caring tone, and try not to become angry or frustrated, or tempted to attack his girlfriend with insults or name-calling. He needs to know that what you're saying is coming from a place of love, not hate.

Hopefully he'll listen to you – but don't be too disheartened if he doesn't. Just think of that time when you tried to warn your best friend about that weird guy she was dating: all the red flags were there, and everyone could see them ... except her. She agreed, nodded along and thanked you, but she still did what she wanted to do. It was only after spending more time with him that she eventually realised the truth herself.

Yes, much of her pain could have been avoided if she'd listened to you in the first place. Ignoring well-intentioned advice can sometimes mean real damage gets done later on. But, sometimes, people need to make their own mistakes and come to the realisation themselves before they see the situation clearly and do something about it.

And, let's be honest – have you always listened to every warning you've received about someone you were dating? Yeah, I didn't think so.

Your brother might be the same. If he wants to continue with his girlfriend, then, unfortunately, you'll have to allow him the space to do so. There's only so much you can do. Your brother is the one who gets to make these choices about his own life, and if he's really stubborn about this girl, you don't want to wind up causing a rift between the two of you that can't be healed or means that he won't listen to you in the future.

If she really is bad news, then you have to have faith that in time your brother will see her for what she is.

Brown Girl Wisdom

For anyone who isn't Asian, it can sometimes feel challenging to date a brown girl. You may not understand why certain things are the way they are – and if you feel super lost, you should ask your girlfriend about why things are the way they are. Respect her answers. She knows it might not be what you're used to, but if you care about her, you can make it work.

For anyone dating a brown girl, here are some tips to help:

- Do not expect to be 'claimed'. She will not be posting pictures or shouting from the rooftops that you're hers. Don't take it personally – she's not embarrassed. She's not hiding the fact that she's dating *you*. She's hiding that she's dating *at all*.
- Prepare to sneak around. It will feel like you're having an affair. You might sincerely think she's trying to hide from her other boyfriend. But she's not. She's trying to hide from the Aunties.
- Accept that it will be a *long* while before you meet the parents. She will probably meet your parents several times over before she even admits to her own parents that you exist.

- Know that mid-week meet-ups aren't easy. And when they do happen, they're usually with a bag of McDonald's and some awkward kissing in the back of the car.
- Book hotels for nights in alone. You will *not* get a nice night in together at her house – not without a family member walking in every two minutes to offer you a plate of *chaat* and samosas.
- Expect to get a dry mouth. It'll develop over time, from all the conversations you whisper your way through so no one hears you on the phone.
- Realise that meeting the parents will feel a lot like a job interview, with a stream of questions to answer. Treat it like a job interview: make sure to stay polite, answer the questions without waffling too much – oh, and dress that little bit smarter than normal.
- If you do meet the family, expect to be asked when you're getting married. After all, she's been keeping it a secret for so long because it's only safe to share when it looks like you have a chance of staying together for ever.
- Learn how to keep any overseas holidays a secret from her side. You probably won't be in each other's pictures – it may look like you went on a solo trip.
- Understand that you may be asked to block members of her family on social media, for privacy and security reasons. It's to keep her safe and it'll make her life much easier.

Follow these tips, and you can expect a long and happy relationship with your special brown girl.

And to my fellow brown girls: if you want to casually date, and figure out the things you like and dislike in potential partners – that's okay. It might not always feel okay, not with the Aunties poking their noses in, but that guilt you feel is the result of an old-fashioned mindset. Breaking those traditions, and dating in a safe and self-aware way, is something to be proud of.

For my brown sisters, here are my key dating dos and don'ts:

- Do be honest with yourself about what you want.
- Don't force yourself into dating if you're not ready for it.
- Do dress how you feel most comfortable, and only agree to date activities you like.
- Don't pretend to be someone you're not, just to impress your date.
- Do explain to your partner that dating brown girls is a bit different.
- Don't let your partner's efforts to adapt go unappreciated.
- Do perfect your secret-keeping skills, *if* you need to hide it from the family.
- Don't tell Auntie. Just . . . don't.
- Do understand that dating is an experience, and doesn't have to be means to an end.
- Don't be afraid to relax, and enjoy.

Dating is a wonderful way of getting to know yourself, above all else. So try not to put so much pressure on yourself to find 'the one', as it just makes the whole experience even more daunting.

Anyway, the reason the Aunties fear casual dating so much is fundamentally nothing to do with dating itself. It's not because they think there's something dangerous about going out for a meal, or holding hands, or even a little kiss on the cheek.

They're not afraid of those things – but they *are* afraid of what those things imply. They're afraid of that one, ultimate thing, above all else. The one thing they believe can ruin an unmarried brown girl for ever.

Sex.

And that's an *entirely* different minefield.

9

'DON'T BE ONE OF THOSE CHEAP GIRLS'

If there is one thing I'm proud to say I've picked up from my Aunties or mum, it's the use of the word 'cheap'.

'She doesn't dress well at all . . . so *cheap.*'

'Listen to how she talks . . . so *cheap.*'

'She didn't even say hello to me, she has no manners . . . so *cheap.*'

Wow. It sure is punchy when said right.

You've got to say it with a shake of the head, and a certain facial expression: your nose scrunched up a little, a slight side-eye. For some reason, when you do all of this and say it in a slight accent, it just hits the spot a little harder for me.

So *cheap.* I can literally feel myself turning into one of the Aunties when I say it like this. But I just love it! It's the ideal way of insulting someone without using profanity. It's the kind of emotional but understated expression where less is so much more. However, I have to say I don't use this term in the same way the Aunties would when they're describing their dislike for a brown girl's dress sense, for example. For me, it's the type of thing you would say when you have left a relative's house and they didn't serve enough food ('so cheap'), when you forgot to offer someone water or tea within the first five minutes of their arrival to your house and are full of embarrassment ('so cheap'), or if you're serving watered-down alcohol to your guests at an Indian wedding ('so cheap'). It's also a term to display disrespect. Dare I say it, these examples are based on real-life events!

Another extreme jibe from the Aunties is the word 'tart'. When used alongside cheap, it's the ultimate insult. Far worse than any profanity. *'Cheap tart.'* It's packed with such a punch, and a level of disdain that no other combination of words can ever quite match. It's the Aunties' own, much more sanitised way of gossiping, rather than using explicit slurs. Still, I would never wish for them to say it about me as it still isn't the most pleasant of terms!

It's pretty much exclusively used when the Aunties are referring to another female, casting judgement on them over things that don't really concern them. The activities that may lead to you being branded a *'cheap tart'* include, but aren't limited to: dressing in an ever-so-slightly revealing way; openly sharing holiday photos where you're with your boyfriend; pool party pics with your girls in bikinis and drinking shots; any situation at all where you're drinking shots; talking too loudly and brashly at family occasions; bringing a new boyfriend to meet everyone; and, of course, anyone knowing that you're not married and have had sex.

As a brown girl, you're not supposed to even know what

sex *is* – at least, not until after you're married. And who knows when that could be?! Who knows whether it'll even happen at all? Not everyone gets married; not everyone has a partner of the opposite sex; not everyone wants kids.

Nevertheless, the unwritten rule for brown girls is: unless you're doing it with the sole intent of reproducing with your husband, sex is forbidden.

It's most likely every South Asian parent's biggest nightmare for their child to get pregnant before they're married. Would their first worry be their daughter's state of mind, or their grandchild's health? Sadly, no. The *first* thing they would worry about is what everyone else is going to say, especially the dreaded Aunties. This kind of news would have every Auntie on the scale talking, and you know they wouldn't be celebrating the new life being brought into the world.

Pregnancy before marriage is reasonably rare in the brown community, but of course it still happens. In a few instances, it's planned, and the brown girl has chosen to become a mother on her own terms. More often, though, it's an accident, and the poor woman is put in a very isolated position. Where can she go for help, if her own parents are going to react with shame rather than support? How can she admit her sex life to them when they refused to even acknowledge that sex is a thing at all?

Most of us know about sex and, crucially,

sexual protection. But we learn about it in school, or perhaps by clicking through articles from online magazines. Our parents and families rarely, if ever, sit us down and tell us about the birds and the bees. When I was ten years old, I was once reading the dictionary to occupy myself while my parents were doing a clear-out (don't ask me why – I guess I was fascinated by learning new vocabulary that day). Innocently flicking through, I came across the word 'condom' and didn't really understand the definition. So, eager to expand my horizons and gain some new knowledge, I asked my parents what it was.

Instead of getting an explanation, or even a child-friendly answer, *or even* something totally made up, I received the look of death and was told off! And that was that.

But if girls aren't taught about their contraceptive options and how they work, then it opens them up to the risk of a manipulative man taking advantage of their ignorance, which can (ironically enough) lead to unwanted pregnancies and the accompanying psychological burden that comes with them.

In our community, we're never frank and open about sex, its importance and its consequences. Even as a grown woman, I don't think I could even say the word 'sex' in front of my family without feeling an intense wave of shame. It's quite simply not something you're supposed to know about – or learn about, or explore, or watch when it's portrayed on TV, or even *think* about until it's the 'right time'.

Bear in mind, all of these rules seem to apply only to women. In theory, the men are supposed to obey too, and stay abstinent before marriage. But in practice, the same male family members who shame you for losing your virginity before marriage will be the ones taking trips to Amsterdam to head down the red light district.

Yep, the double standards are real.

It's fine for the boys – they can run off and get up to whatever they like, without the fear of being called a *'cheap tart'*. But what are we brown girls supposed to do? We also have our own desires and curiosities, and have just as much right to explore our bodies and our attractions. It's fair to say that sex is far less taboo in Western culture than in brown communities. We're constantly reminded in TV shows and in Hollywood films how normal it is to be intimate with someone, that there isn't anything 'wrong' with sex, and this can create a tension between the Western culture we're surrounded by and what our parents teach us or expect of us.

These things are perfectly normal and healthy, and these days, sex education is on the school curriculum for adolescents in Western countries. This is important, as girls need to understand their bodies, how hormones work, and about sex. Regarding these topics as taboo is a mistake. Learning about our bodies and that masturbation is standard practice for some and not something to feel guilty about is a powerful way to take away feelings of shame that can be prevalent among girls and young women in the brown community.

Knowledge is power, and our young brown girls need to have knowledge of their own physicality. Too many of them have no notion of the agency they have over their own bodies. Consent is one of the most vital aspects of sex, if not arguably *the* most important, and it's rightly being taught by Western schools more and more.

Sadly, in the brown community, the generally held view is that marriage *is* consent – meaning a woman can't have sex before she becomes a wife, but is then all but obligated to sleep with her husband whenever he feels like it after they're man and wife. It's vital to teach the brown community that consent is much more nuanced than that, and needs to be given by all parties. Consent must be enthusiastic, and free of coercion, and above all it must be respected. Without a healthy grasp of that knowledge, by both sexes, we condemn too many brown women and girls to rape and abuse.

At the same time, some of us may decide we genuinely do want to wait until marriage before we have sex – not due to societal standards or duress, but because, after learning all the facts and options, that's what we've decided we want to do. But what do we do when all the Western people around us can't even conceive of the idea?

Let's talk about sex.

Brown Girl Problems

'I left my house at 3 a.m., through the back door and out the side gate, to go and have sex.'

Okay. I'll start out by admitting that, personally, I've not felt the urgency to leave my house for such activities at that kind of small hour of the night. But, sis, hand on heart – if your needs were calling, then who am I to judge?!

We unmarried brown girls are all meant to walk around like pure, innocent virgins. We're supposed to have no concept of sex whatsoever. Right?

I don't understand why Asians keep up this narrative. We all know where the Kama Sutra comes from.

But the story lives on. So when a brown girl decides she is curious about sex or has desires that need to be met, she has to be very careful with how she goes about it.

For anyone that has never dated a brown person before (and, obviously, I'm particularly focusing on brown girls), I'm sorry to tell you that the reality of it doesn't exactly resemble how it goes in the movies.

Ideally:

You meet. You start talking. You go on a few dates, wherever you want. When you're both ready, and comfortable, you have sex. You enjoy the time you spend together, and you seek out more of it. And so it continues. At some point, you'll meet the parents. You take your relationship at your own pace, until you want or feel the need to get married.

Now, let me describe what dating a brown girl is like:

You meet. You might go on a couple of dates, or you might go to a drive through to hang out and chat in private. Then, when you're actually 'dating', and ready to get serious, you have a couple of options. Going out for dinner and the cinema all the time soon adds up, you know – and you both finally want to spend time together somewhere more private. So now, you have to get a little creative.

Option one. Hotel rooms. This can get expensive, and isn't exactly sustainable every single night. But you do get reassurance that the Aunties won't catch you together.

Hopefully, you won't get seen by anyone and snitched on to your parents, so you can just have a normal night in. And who doesn't want that once in a while?

Option two. You're down a side road, with the both of you in the backseat of your car. Now, this isn't necessarily as dirty as it sounds ... You just needed somewhere quiet, just the two of you. You know. A moment to talk. Just talk.

Having to sneak out of the house probably makes her feel a bit guilty, and possibly resentful. It must be hard when your parents are smiling at you the next morning over breakfast, and asking if you slept well. It's never fun to hide things from your family.

But at the same time, why *should* you have to hide anything? You're not doing anything wrong – you're a consenting, responsible adult, in charge of your own decisions. Your family should respect that.

Many brown girls are sexually active, especially those leaning towards Wild West tendencies. The straightforward truth is, it's a perfectly normal and natural part of wanting to develop a more intimate bond with your partner. A lot of Wild West and On-the-Fence brown girls share the prevalent Western view that sex is an important tester of compatibility with someone, and therefore is better explored before marriage.

And what about By-the-Book brown girls? Are we supposed to believe they're all happily abstinent, with no sexual curiosity or desires at all? Are we supposed to believe they're sitting at home, all night, every night, invisible chastity belts locked until marriage, praying to God to say thanks for their flawless purity?

Yeah, right.

The By-the-Book brown girls have needs just as much as the rest of us. And, sometimes, their needs win out. In fact, they're probably the ones most likely to be sneaking out at 3 a.m. – how else can they possibly even entertain the idea of having a sex life? They're also the ones having to come up with the most creative lies and stories, because 'I was hanging out with a friend' isn't going to cut it. It's perfectly fair enough – when you haven't yet met the man you think you might marry, it's only natural to be a little impatient. And you can't deny your body for ever.

But don't bother explaining any of that to the Aunties. It will *not* fly.

Unfortunately, pre-marital sex is just too prickly a subject for many Asian families still. It can lead to serious and extreme consequences, from being kicked out of the house to being estranged from your family altogether. While a Mild Auntie might just about accept that not all unmarried brown girls are virgins, a Spicy Auntie will loudly proclaim her condemnation of any woman who would bring such shame on her family. And, meanwhile, a Hot Auntie will do her best to make sure you're banned from entering the house, or possibly the country, ever again.

Does that mean a brown girl should deny herself her own needs and wants? No, it doesn't. But it does mean you have to tread very carefully.

If you're leaving the house at 3 a.m., make sure you're safe – nothing is worth putting yourself in danger for. That goes for ensuring you're physically safe, by never finding yourself alone in the dark, as well as sexually safe, by using appropriate methods to lower the risks of STI transmission and pregnancy.

However, as long as you're looking after yourself, then I can completely appreciate that, sometimes, the risk is worth it to get your needs met *and* keep the family in blissful ignorance.

'I met a white guy and he seems really nice. When do I tell him I'm waiting till marriage?'

It's very easy to think that this is the first thing you need to tell him. And on the other hand, it's very easy to never ever want to mention it.

I understand. You're growing a nice bond together. You have a good time, you make each other laugh and you share the same interests. You can see potential for a future with this guy.

However, he may have certain expectations that you just can't provide. You don't want to 'let him down', as such, later down the line. So it's constantly on your mind; it's the massive elephant in the room that won't leave you alone.

And yet, the prospect of telling him is a bit terrifying, especially if you really like him. You might worry that it'll be a deal-breaker, and that he'll lose all interest in you as soon as he knows.

Living in a Western society can come with these pressures.

We generally get the sense that we'll have a much less difficult life if we're more like everyone else – our friends and peers who surround us the most. Even if they themselves come from different backgrounds, we always want to make sure we have more in common with them than not.

And sex, regardless of whether you yourself want to have it, is an important factor to many people, especially in the West. It's true that some people won't want to pursue a relationship if they realise there won't be sexual activity attached.

Many young brown girls can be pushed into believing they need to give in to those pressures. There's a general anxiety that if they don't, they'll always be the weird one who never quite fits in.

This affects all of us – Wild West, On-the-Fence and By-the-Book. No matter how comfortable or uncomfortable we feel with particular Western traditions and expectations, we will always be brown girls. Of course we're proud of that, but it does mean, in Western contexts, that we won't always fully fit in. We'll often be the only one in the room who looks like we do. Sometimes, we may be the only one in the room who believes what we believe.

At those times, a little voice in the back of our heads can start to emerge. It's annoying, and persistent, and it can take over our lives.

It just whispers, *Do it. Do it.* No matter whether we're comfortable or not. *Do it.* We don't want to be the weird one, do we? We don't want to be the lone voice in the room. We don't want to drive a potential partner away. We don't want to be alone. *Do it.*

But I think to be able to make this decision for yourself and stick with it is a beautiful, brave thing. To not be affected by those pressures takes a lot of strength. But it's so, so worth it.

If you want to stay a virgin until you feel the time is right, that is okay. If you have sex, when you have sex, and who you want to have sex with, are absolutely no one's decisions but your own. Ignore the voice saying *do it*. You'll do it if and when you feel ready and comfortable, and not a moment before.

The exact same is true for when you want to tell this guy that you're waiting for marriage. You'll tell him if and when you feel ready, and comfortable.

The truth is, though, there's a chance it will get brought up by him first. What to do if that happens?

Do the same as when you bring it up in your own time: be completely honest. Don't pretend to be someone you're not. Don't try to hide your stance from him, and don't attempt to convince him that you're comfortable when you're seriously not. Tell him you're waiting until marriage, and you're content with your choice.

What happens then?

A lot of things may happen. I hate to say it, but he may back away.

If he does, there are some key things for you to remember. It might be that you got on well, but if he can't accept this about you, then he wasn't actually 'the one' after all.

If sex is a vital part of a romantic relationship to him, then try not to judge that – he's allowed to have his own non-negotiables. Hopefully, if he's a genuinely good guy, you can still stay friends and be in each other's lives, even if you're not soulmates.

If he immediately cuts you out of his life altogether ... well, then, he was clearly only after one thing from you. *Definitely* not worth your time.

Don't feel disheartened, though. Yes, he might decide it won't work out. But he might decide the opposite.

Wanting to wait to have sex until marriage, while perhaps more common in the Asian community than in the Western one, is still not exclusive to just one culture. He may surprise you – it may be that he's waiting for marriage, too.

Or, it may be that it wasn't what he was expecting, but he's willing to wait – for you.

The right person, and a good person, will always respect your wishes, no matter whether he shares the same personal views as you or not. If he's worth your time, then he'll know you're worth his time, too. He will wait for you because you mean more to him than sex.

There's one more thing to keep in mind. You've decided to wait until marriage – that's completely admirable and should be respected by everyone. There may be one day, though, where you find you might be changing your mind – not due to external pressures or coercion, but because you feel something shifting in yourself.

Remember that that's okay, too. Some people do feel happiest waiting until marriage; others' beliefs may change over time. If yours do change, don't beat yourself up. It's natural to feel guilty about it, like you're going back on your word, but the reality is the only person you need to stay true to is yourself.

Every choice you make takes you on your own journey, which you, and only you, should have full control of.

Meet your own expectations. No one else's.

'I'm scared no one will marry me if I'm not a virgin.'

One of the biggest problems to do with brown girls and sex is that so many brown girls may want to explore their sexuality – but they're filled with an intense, crippling fear of doing so. This doesn't just come from the gossiping and judgemental Aunties, but from the men in our cultures too. They can sometimes be even worse than the Hot Auntie we dread.

Why do young brown boys get a free pass? Why is it okay for a brown boy to have experience – often a *lot* of it – in this department, yet be so critical about the young women in their community who might consider doing the same? I'm not saying we brown girls need to be just like the boys and go and get our body count up. However, if we did wish to do so, who is anyone else to judge? Especially when there's such ridiculous levels of hypocrisy involved.

Let's forget about the actual act of sex for a minute. We brown girls are afraid to show it simply when we *feel* sexy. Taking a picture that makes us feel attractive can be shameful – and I don't even mean full-on nudes. You could be pouting a little too much more than the Aunties like, or maybe your top is cut slightly low and just reveals a quarter of a centimetre of cleavage. Even *that* is unacceptable. The Aunties, and the men, and it feels like practically everyone, will dismiss you as a *cheap tart* – never mind if you've never even held hands with a guy. Showing the world that we look or feel sexy comes with great shame.

Someone is always going to think what you're doing is inappropriate – even the smallest, most innocent of things. If we're shamed and alienated for minor misdeeds like those, then having sex is something we should be completely and utterly disgraced by. Right?

It's wrong, and it's unfair. We brown girls are incredible people. We know good humour from dealing with our crazy Aunties. We're smart and savvy from navigating the complexity of hiding things from our parents. We're beautiful, with the most amazing hair and skin and features. We're each of us unique, with our own wonderful and varied personalities.

Should we wish to get married, then each and every one of us is an amazing person that a partner would be lucky to spend their lives with. Why should sex suddenly take all that away?

Being a virgin or not has no impact on who you are. Of course it may change some of the ways you feel within yourself, but it shouldn't change the way anyone else sees you.

I can fully, wholly appreciate the worry that having sex will make men not want to marry you. But let me reframe that belief into something more truthful: having sex will make *unworthy* men not want to marry you. Men who are hypocritical, and judgemental, and misogynistic in their views that women have to conform to rigid standards in order to be valuable. Think about it – do you want to spend your life with a man like that? You're much better off without that kind of hassle.

The men who reject a woman for having sex should be rejected right back. The men who are understanding, and know that a woman is so much more than her sex life, are the ones worth sticking with.

I personally believe we women are precious, and sacred, in many ways. I believe our virginity is something to only lose when we're 100 per cent sure and ready. Maybe that's within marriage, and maybe it's not. Maybe it's never.

But we should have the choice, and the right, to do what we wish to do without the fear of being judged. None of the decisions we make with respect to our own sex lives determines whether or not we're the perfect candidate for marriage.

'I pretended hickeys were a crazy rash spreading all over my body when my mum saw.'

How do I describe what a 'hickey' is to an Auntie? It's not a rash, it's not a burn. No, a vampire hasn't come and attacked me in the night.

It's a *love bite*, Auntie.

I bet even that doesn't explain it, as they've probably never had 'love' expressed to them in that way before – through bites. I hope *not*, actually. I don't like the idea of my Auntie taking part in such misbehaviour any more than she would like the idea of me doing it.

Brown girl or not, in my opinion, hickeys, love bites, or whatever else you want to call them, are a big no. To me, hickeys are another thing the Aunties would call *'cheap'*, and I would have to agree with them.

I can't sit here on my high horse and act as if I've never been in your position, though. I actually once told my mum that my skin had got caught in my zip, hence the mark. As I keep saying, it's second nature for us brown girls to expertly hide things and keep secrets.

Look, I understand if you're in a moment of passion, I honestly do. But is there really any need to go that far? Isn't it all a bit public, a bit in-your-face? (Or a bit on-your-neck, I guess.)

As I've grown older, I've realised that there are other ways for love, passion and affection to be expressed. I think it's something you do when you're young because it's exciting, you're 'making your mark', and it feels like something to quietly brag about. *Look at my hickey – I'm a grown-up now!*

I would never police the safe and consensual actions of any adult – you do you, always. But I'll do me, too. Once I realised how ridiculous it looked when at school, college, work and, crucially, at home, the shame was enough to put me off showing or receiving affection in that way.

And anyway – if you're trying to hide your activities from the Aunties, hickeys are the number-one way to do the opposite.

'I caught an STI, but I'm too scared to go to the clinic in case anyone sees me.'

We've all been there. Maybe we haven't all had a sexually transmitted infection, but we've all had that pang of dread when we've felt a little itch in our private area. And we all know a visit to the sexual health clinic is never something to look forward to.

Contracting an STI is frightening enough. On top of that, being too afraid or ashamed to see a doctor just adds to the pressure, and so I can imagine your head is swimming with horrible thoughts:

What if I bump into an Auntie?

What if she asks me why I'm there?

What if she tells my parents?

I know it's scary, but I'd advise you to keep following that train of thought. Think it all the way through. Because soon you'll realise:

Hold on a minute . . . why would Auntie be at the sexual health clinic too?!

I promise you: if there's an Auntie, a cousin, or someone else you know at the same clinic you're visiting, this will probably be the only time they *won't* want to spark up a conversation with you. At all.

Auntie will throw her shawl over herself, trying to disguise her face as best as she can. If it's your cousin, she's immediately putting her hoodie up and suddenly shoving some sunglasses on, keeping it very low-key.

Of course, they could be at the sexual health clinic for any number of reasons. They could be getting testing or treatment for an STI, or they could be there to discuss family planning options, or methods of contraception. It could be anything. But there is no way they'll be up for having a friendly, open chat about it with you. So maybe, just maybe, this is the one time you don't have to worry about Auntie telling the entire world about your business.

An STI is just like any other virus we might catch. It's unfortunate that we can only catch them in intimate circumstances, because it can add an extra layer of embarrassment when you go to get it treated. We have to jump through hurdles, keeping our appointments a secret, and have to mentally build up the strength and courage to speak to a doctor about it. More often than not, we have to do it all alone. And this isn't just for brown girls – the stigma affects pretty much all young women. So much so that I think the fear of being known for having an STI is even worse than having the STI itself!

So, don't be hard on yourself, and don't feel like you're alone. Although none of us wants to catch one, STIs aren't uncommon, and many people have to deal with them – yes, even other brown girls. We just don't hear about it. If you're able to confide in someone close to you, like a trusted sibling or a friend, I can assure you, it will take some of the pressure off and make you feel less alone. You never know, they could have experienced something similar, or know someone that knows someone with the same story and, all of a sudden, you won't feel so alienated any more.

It can happen even if we are careful and take preventative measures (although they significantly reduce the chances of catching one) and, tragically, sometimes a woman may contract an STI after non-consensual activity. Having an STI doesn't make you some irresponsible harlot. Everyone's situation is different, and no one has the right to judge. Maybe that's why this is the one time Auntie knows it's better to keep her head down and her mouth shut.

I know you're feeling scared and ashamed, but I have to stress that it's so, so, *so* important for you to go to your GP or a sexual health doctor to get this seen to as soon as possible. Delaying will only make it worse, which could badly affect your long-term health. So book an appointment now.

If you live at home with family, I know that can be easier said than done. I know from living at home myself that whenever I'm going anywhere, there are always a lot of questions. Where am I going? Who am I going with? When will I be back? I know our families ask us all these questions because they care, but being interrogated like this adds a lot of stress to an already stressful situation.

Try to pick an appointment time when your parents are out at work, or going to be somewhere else. That will make it much easier to be discreet, and you won't have to directly lie to them. But if there's no way of sneaking out of the house without anyone knowing, then it's time to employ one of our old faithful cover stories about going to a friend's house. Get the details firmly in your mind before you head out, so you're not making it up on the spot. And ensure it's a trusted friend, and you give them a heads up – just in case your parents call them to check on you. If that friend can accompany you for moral support, then even better.

At the end of the day, it's important to know exactly who you're about to be intimate with and to use safe sex methods such as condoms to reduce the risks of contracting STIs (or getting pregnant, for that matter!). Don't ever be afraid to ask your partner about their sexual history, and when they last had a sexual health check-up. It might feel a bit awkward, but it's vital – it's for your own safety and health.

Brown Girl Wisdom

Let's be real: we're in the twenty-first century, but sometimes it can feel like we're in the 1800s, or earlier, when it comes to a topic like sex. I can barely believe I'm actually writing about this, if I'm honest. I am definitely scared about what my Aunties are going to say.

Still, I believe we need to talk about these things openly, instead of pretending it's not happening.

Sex is not something to be ashamed of. We're supposed to build and nurture relationships with each other, and when it comes to romantic relationships, sex is often a vital part of one. Consensual sex is so important in many people's relationships; having that connection with someone can make or break a spark.

It's imprinted in our biology. Denying our bodies' needs is denying what makes us human. It's why discovering what physical sensations and actions we enjoy, whether with a partner or by ourselves, is a healthy and normal thing.

And for the brown girls that want to wait until they're married – don't let Western society, or anyone else, tell you any different. It's okay to be a virgin; no one should ever have sex before they're ready and comfortable, and rushing into it due to other people's expectations is never worth it.

It's okay *not* to be a virgin, too. It doesn't make you less worthy or less respectable. It doesn't mean no one will want to marry you any more.

The important thing is that you are doing things on your own terms, in your own time. If you are, then there's nothing to feel guilty about at all.

I'm not saying we need to be shouting from the rooftops about our sex lives. I do agree that some things should remain private, because they are personal. A sexual relationship between two people is fundamentally between those two people, and that's it – it doesn't concern anyone else.

But there's a big difference between privacy and secrecy. When you decide to keep something on the down-low because of your own personal preferences, that's more than fair. But when you're *forced* to keep quiet, pushed into a place where admitting what you're doing or what you're thinking would get you ostracised, then that's altogether much more dangerous.

Brown girls grow up with the perception of sex being dirty. It's intrinsically something to be ashamed of. You're taught about the perils of fraternising with boys, wearing short skirts, being a *cheap tart*. You're taught there's no going back – walk down that path and you'll be marked for ever.

It's drilled into your brain: sex before marriage is wrong. You're not married? Then, *sex is wrong*.

So you go along with this, even if you don't really want to deep down. You believe what you're told, and decide you won't have sex before you're married.

But what happens *after* you're married?

After years and years of having fingers wagged at you, heads shaken at you, everyone telling you that sex is basically the worst thing on the planet and doing it makes you next to worthless – how are you meant to instantly switch? Are you supposed to feel differently about it now, just because you have a ring on your finger?

First-time sex is a bit terrifying for anyone, but it won't be remotely appealing if it's never once been presented in a positive light before. It will end up being something that is always shrouded in shame, even if it's suddenly become the 'right time' to do it. Brown girls can't have a happy and healthy attitude towards sex if they're never taught that this is a possibility.

I strongly believe this is something we need to be more open and honest about. We can teach brown girls, as they grow, that sex isn't something to be scared of. It's healthy and completely, 100 per cent normal to feel curious and to want to explore these urges. The fact that we feel sexual impulses and desires shouldn't be a big secret that we're all too petrified to ever discuss.

Nor is it something to rush into. It's a new and close level of intimacy with another person, so it's a step that should only be taken when you're ready to, free of any coercion or peer pressure.

Sex can be beautiful, and meaningful. So take your time, respect your own needs as well as your partner's, and remember that it's a wholly personal thing, between the two of you.

Sex doesn't have to be a secret. It's just no one's business but your own.

10

'YOU NEED TO SETTLE DOWN'

I wonder, when exactly is 'too late'?

Is there a particular age where suddenly you go from still having time left, to it being 'too late'? Is it your early twenties? Is twenty-five the year it becomes too late, or do we get a couple more years afterwards? Is it twenty-eight-and-a-half? Maybe it happens overnight, and then, boom, you're done. Too late. But we all know it's *definitely* before we turn thirty.

Right?

Even if we ignore when exactly this is supposed to happen, there are still so many questions. 'Too late' for what? What exactly do those words mean?

And if the time of 'too late' comes and goes, what happens to you then?

Let's try to understand all this.

I'll start with how your elders imagine the timeline of your life panning out.

You're born – wahey! (Well, in some cases, it's met with disappointment if you turn out to be a little girl rather than a little boy. But we'll get on to that a bit later.)

You're then expected to focus on your studies, and your studies alone. No speaking to boys, no boyfriends, no dating – you do not have time for any of that nonsense, because education is *life*.

You then educate yourself further at university, get a degree, and that helps to get you a job. Then, voila, now is the 'right' age to get married.

You thought education was life? Turns out, now, *marriage* is life. Huh. That sure came around suddenly.

I think there's a particular drive for brown women to get married as soon as possible, because in brown cultures, marriage isn't just marriage – it's a symbol of true adulthood. When you're married, there's a shift in how society perceives you. You're no longer a child. You don't have to live solely in accordance with your parents' wishes any more.

As an Asian kid, this appeals a *lot*.

Growing up, if I asked my parents' permission to do anything even vaguely independent, I always got the same answer.

'Mum, Dad, can I go on a holiday with my friends?'

'After you're married.'

'Mum, Dad, can I get a tattoo?'

'Once you get married.'

'Mum, Dad, I'd like to go backpacking alone.'

'As long as it's when you're married, then you can go with him.'

Once I became someone's wife, I'd have the approval my husband, so then everything would be okay. In other words, I could only pursue the fun things that I wanted to do for myself if I had a man in my life to give me a thumbs up first.

I think these blanket 'as soon as you're married' responses I received are part of the reason I wanted to 'rebel' in the first place. I say 'rebel' but, in the grand scheme of things, I genuinely don't think I was all that bad. For example, when I was in college, I would go to the local high street with my friends and somehow always come back with a new ear piercing. *That* kind of 'rebelling'.

Still, every time I returned home with a new hoop glinting at my ear, my mum would say nothing. But she'd give me *the look*. You know the one I mean. It's that death stare your parents give you that says a thousand words. It's the same look you get when you're at a family event and you just so happen to say a little too much, or tell the wrong joke and make your parents look like they've taught you nothing. *That* look.

It wasn't like I enjoyed getting *the look*; I didn't want to make my mum and dad angry. I just wanted to prove a point. I was going to do what I wanted to do, for me, without a man and without marriage. If I think about it, a lot of the decisions I've made in my life have been down to that reason.

I was able to 'rebel' and follow my own path, and show that I didn't need a husband to do what I wanted. But many brown girls, especially those By-the-Book ones who don't want to rock the boat, wind up being desperate to get married quickly so they can finally explore some of their own opportunities for independence. Where I reacted by doubling down, other brown girls might internalise the pressure. Which is part of why, as soon as your education and income are sorted, the switch to focusing on marriage is so instantaneous.

Now, being fair here, I would say there has been some significant progression with all this. The older generation aren't quite so anxious about it as they used to be, back when being an unmarried girl at nineteen was considered over the hill. Although you may be desperate for independence, you're afforded more flexibility now than you may have once been. You've now got a little more time to breathe, compared to how things were in the past.

Now you can get married in your late twenties (perhaps). Amazing!

But still, just make sure it's before you hit the big *three-oh*. After that, there is absolutely no way of stopping the Aunties from throwing their intrusive questions at you.

For me, getting closer to thirty and being unmarried feels like the walls are closing in, the sand is slipping through the hourglass quicker, and I'll have absolutely no hope left once I get there. During the course of my life, and especially the past few years, I've heard comments such as 'You'll be on the shelf', implying that if you're still single at thirty, you're basically like something in the supermarket that's gone past its sell-by date.

I've been told that being on my own and openly independent looks like too much fun, so it's intimidating for a guy to approach me. I'm not really sure what I'm supposed

to do instead, look sad and lonely? It's hard enough being a woman who's trying to be a boss babe, driving my career forward and making a name for myself, but now I have to deal with these unwanted pressures and insecurities. As much as I try to block out the voices of the Aunties, there's always a concern in the back of my mind: the older I get, the more likely it'll result in my being unwanted by a man.

As I approach thirty, I honestly feel like I'm in panic-buying mode, desperately looking for a guy who is 'marriage material', and trying to get it done as soon as I physically can. And I'm not the only brown girl in her late twenties doing it, either. Finding a husband now is like trying to buy toilet roll during a pandemic lockdown!

Hmm. So the *guy* gets to be the in-demand, almost always sold-out product wanted by everyone, while all the girls are left sitting on the shelf, past their expiry dates. Fantastic.

So I guess we're all supposed to get a move on, and get someone to put a ring on it, right now. The clock's ticking, after all.

Let's be honest and address what no one wants to say out loud: this is all about fertility. They're going by the timing of when they believe our eggs are going to shrivel up and no longer be capable of making a mini me. In which case, the *biological* clock's ticking, after all.

This isn't only a preoccupation in the brown community, of course. Young women of all races and cultures experience this pressure to have kids earlier rather than later. But while Western communities are beginning to champion the validity of alternative paths – such as adoption, single parenting or intentional childlessness – the value brown communities across the world place on a woman still often directly corresponds to her childbearing capacity. There is certainly more of an expectation for us to have kids, and to have them fast.

Now, I understand our families are concerned about our ovaries being ripe so we can have children, but why does getting married have to be the be-all and end-all? Or even having children? Surely that's a choice we get to make for our own lives and our own bodies? Some women may not be *able* to get pregnant. Are they already 'on the shelf'? And what about those of us who may not *want* to get married? Many Western women increasingly reject the institution altogether, seeing it as old-fashioned and patriarchal. Having children out of wedlock isn't very common in brown communities, but is this because we're simply afforded less freedom to stray away from the conventional route?

Sadly, all of those considerations don't mean there isn't that pressure from family, even if it's just the slightest bit. You just know when you attend a family wedding, there's going to be at least one Auntie asking you what your situation is, if you've found a boy, and when you're getting married. They want to know that it's your wedding they'll be going to next.

There's so much to think about, though; you're not just 'running out of time'; you're trying to make sure he's the right person, who fits all the criteria. Who might this man be? How can you possibly find him with the so-called clock ticking?!

Well, if you're a typical brown girl, you have your secret boyfriend, of course! The one you've always insisted was never your boyfriend, just your friend-who-is-a-boy. No problem there. Husband: sorted. Well, provided your family find him suitable. Whoever may be suitable to you might not be suitable to them, unfortunately. In a brown family, it's not just the two of you that get married; it's your whole entire big fat Asian family.

But let's say you've made it to the point where you've found the perfect guy, and even your family's happy, and everything seems to have aligned. Finally, nothing else can go wrong.

Can it?

What scares me is that when I do find 'the one' and I say I want to get married, the wedding planning isn't exactly going to go how it does in the movies.

Indian weddings are competitive. Each one has to top the last wedding you went to. And there's not exactly a flash mob of dancers who are freely available to come to every single wedding and perform the exact same routine. Even if that's what happens in Bollywood movies.

Sigh, Bollywood has really sold us some dreams.

Aside from that, the vast majority of the time, your guest list isn't actually up to you, unless you're paying for the wedding. And even then, someone will have something to say. You'll still have people to please, and not let down.

The people your parents will be adamant about attending your wedding include:

Your dad's brother's mechanic

The corner shop 'Uncle' – much like the Auntie who's not actually your Auntie

Your grandma's sister's best friend

The random couple your parents met last week at someone else's wedding

(Did I mention these are all based on true events?)

Oh, and let's not forget, you've never once met any of the above. *Not once.* And after your wedding, you never will again. Hell, you might not even meet them *during* the wedding.

As I mentioned previously, I'm one of four siblings, and the other three are now married. All three times we have tried to plan the weddings, it's been the same discussions. Arguments over who ought to be invited and who shouldn't be. Somehow, with each wedding there are always new random people to add to the list.

You may have clicked that all my siblings being married includes my brother – my *younger* brother. But honestly, this really isn't a big deal for me. We're only one year apart, so it was always going to be a possibility that this could happen. But ever since he got engaged, if I collected a penny for every time someone told me, 'Just you left now!' – well, I think I would be a millionaire.

It sounds innocent enough, but this compulsion to match up every last brown girl with a brown guy can lead to much darker consequences. In some highly conservative brown communities, forced marriages take place, often with very young girls being made to marry much older men. The girls' happiness and health aren't even considered; instead, they're seen as only good for having children. The highest numbers of forced marriages happen in Pakistan, Bangladesh, Somalia and India, but they happen in Western countries too, with the UK's Forced Marriage Unit handling hundreds of cases every year despite the practice being illegal.

When communities are willing to commit violence and break the law, it's apparent just how dangerous these rigid concepts of marriage and children are. The most orthodox brown communities practically see the two as synonymous: marriage means children, and children mean marriage. You cannot have one without the other. In these societies and for some families, a newly married couple going more than a few months without announcing a pregnancy is seen as unusual. Not always, but it does happen. There'd be whispers of infertility, or an affair.

If a man turns out to be infertile, it's generally regarded that the couple simply has to accept it and live their lives. It doesn't seem to matter whether the woman wants children or not – it's the man's circumstances which dictate the future. In contrast, if it transpires that the woman is infertile, more often than not she will be seen as 'damaged goods' and swiftly divorced. Sure, there are other routes you could take, such as adoption and IVF, although neither are very common and, just like everything else in South Asian culture, they're not openly spoken about.

In any brown community, divorce isn't particularly common. Some families still have extremely dated ideas on divorce and the perceived stigma associated with it, and they are reluctant to support any brown girls considering it as an option. In the more extreme cases, among particularly old-fashioned brown communities, a divorce happens only once in a blue moon, and if it does occur, it's rarely initiated by the woman, although it does happen in certain circumstances such as when there is domestic violence.

However, it would be the man deciding to move on, usually likely because his wife has been accused of infertility or infidelity. Both of these are seen as heinous crimes against marriage. Once this woman's husband has left her, she probably won't be remotely protected by anyone, including those within her own family.

I'm grateful that I was born into the family and community I was. We have the freedom to rejoice in big, glamorous weddings, where the bride and groom are truly happy and in love. We live in a country where gay marriage is legal, and even though the brown community struggles with deep-seated homophobia, there are still cases of brown LGBTQ+ people enjoying their own extravagant wedding ceremonies. In my community, brown girls aren't forced to marry. Some girls are choosing not to marry, or not to have kids. And although divorce is still hugely frowned upon, it's slowly becoming a more viable option for the brown girls who need it, as understanding from their families in this area is growing. I am proud to see brown girls today fighting for their rights, their safety and their happiness, and not tolerating being disrespected.

But there is still a generally entrenched view that marriage and children go hand in hand, within the confines of a heteronormative relationship between two fertile people. Those women who stray from that path are seen as either rebellious or fundamentally flawed.

It's the same thinking that affects the more strict brown communities. It's the same ideals, the same unbending concepts of what's normal and what's not. The fact that some communities accept unforgivable levels of abuse and violence and mine doesn't, doesn't absolve it of its biased attitudes. No, we don't have the same scale of problems, and we're lucky for that – but we still have problems, and it would be dangerous to deny it.

In my view, the issues primarily stem from the idea that there's a default way of doing things, and that anything which slightly deviates from that is bad and wrong. However, something being commonplace or traditional doesn't automatically make it right for everyone. Although some people may genuinely want to get married when they're young and have kids quickly, for many of us it doesn't appeal at all. That doesn't make us wrong. It just makes us different.

There's a lot to tackle. Conformity has long been celebrated in brown communities, but I believe it's time for that to stop. Marriage and children are too important, too life-changing, to be based on such archaic ideas.

Brown Girl Problems

'I'm in love with someone who has a child. How will my family accept him?'

To a lot of Western people, this will seem like an insane, unnecessary question. Why shouldn't your family accept him? Just because a person has a child, does it mean they don't deserve to be loved or accepted?

Unfortunately, in brown families, dating someone who has a child from a previous relationship is a huge no-no.

Trying to accept someone else's child can be really difficult for most brown families. This is partly the reason so many don't adopt. There's a long-held focus on upholding the integrity of the family bloodline in Asian cultures. Many things are accused of ruining that integrity, whether it's true or not. There are often unfounded worries that this poor, innocent child will carry deficiencies in their blood. And some people might believe that the child will 'taint' the purity of their own union with the man – after all, they are living proof he's had a life, including a sex life, with someone before them.

Brown families never seem to put themselves in someone else's shoes.

And honestly, I'm not trying to condemn them. In fact, I can really relate to this, as I used to have a bias against dating men with kids. I used to believe it'd be preferable to date a guy who didn't have all that history. I especially thought I'd have no time for men who'd become fathers outside of marriage. 'I'm sure he's a nice man, but he clearly has no sense of self-control or responsibility,' I would smugly think to myself, before swiftly moving along.

Then, a couple of years back, the only guys I would ever meet happened to also be fathers. I didn't plan it; it just kept happening, purely by chance. And they were often such lovely, sweet men – maybe not quite right for me, but only down to a lack of chemistry.

It must have been karma, or God's way of teaching me not to be so judgemental about these men just because they'd had children out of wedlock.

Every girl always says, 'No way, I could never be with a baby daddy' – that is, until you start feeling attracted to a baby daddy! At that point, you start to understand how wrong you've been for judging people without giving them a chance to show you who they are. You realise that you've been putting yourself on a bit of a pedestal. I always thought that I couldn't date a man with kids because I've avoided getting pregnant before marriage, and therefore believed my life partner should be of a similar mindset. But this way of thinking just doesn't hold up. It's never fair to assume you know a person's character or beliefs without first giving them the opportunity to express themselves. There are plenty of reasons an unmarried man might have a baby, and they don't necessarily mean he's the wrong man for me or you.

And what about people who have a child from a previous marriage? Sometimes marriages don't work out. Sometimes a partner leaves. Sometimes you leave a partner. Sometimes, tragically, a partner dies. Should all these people who found themselves in circumstances they never dreamed of be discouraged from trying to find romance again?

Unfortunately, I know that, in my own family, dating a man who had a child would make me the talk of the town.

We really need to change our attitudes. We need to stop thinking like our older generations and give people a chance based on who they are, not based on their past or on our own rigid ideals of acceptance.

Not having a child doesn't make you a better person, or more 'pure', than someone who has had a child with someone else, or, at least, it shouldn't. Thankfully, things in the brown community are starting to change, albeit slowly, and second marriages are more commonplace now.

In addition, general attitudes towards being a step-parent have also changed. Once upon a time, it might have been that having a step-child was passively tolerated, rather than actively enjoyed or celebrated. Nowadays, there is increasingly more willingness to make an effort with and accept kids who aren't biologically related to you into the wider family.

My advice is to follow your heart. Only you know if you can love another person's child. It may not be easy straight away, but you might not even have to step in to the role of step-mum. Your role in the child's life might be that of a friend, confidante, another person to turn to. Fundamentally, that's all kids need – a safe space. It might be that you struggle to establish that bond, but you should never feel alone in it. You wouldn't want to lose this man and regret it, but at the same time you need him to be able to fight your corner as much as you'll fight his. He should be there, helping you and his child in forging a relationship.

As for whether your family will accept it, it's hard to say. But my feeling is, if they see you caring for this family as much as your parents care for you, and they know that the relationship you're in makes you happy, then they'll realise that perhaps there's not such a difference after all.

'My boyfriend comes from a single-parent household and it is stereotyped as a broken family. I'm worried my family won't accept him.'

We've spoken about South Asian families having a certain checklist for who is acceptable to marry. When they say a 'good family', this usually comes down to a few things – wealth, education and what they define as *stability*. Part of that, in short, means having both parents married and together.

It *looks* so much better having both parents around, doesn't it? It makes such a lovely, balanced picture for the family photograph; it has such nice connotations of eternal love and a happy home. Because that's apparently what matters – looking good. The image, the idea, and how everyone else is going to perceive your family.

When your parents tell the extended family members about 'the boy', they want to be able to gloat about his background and say brilliant words about them (often with a considerable amount of exaggeration). This is quite normal within Asian families, and in many other communities too. Every parent wants to know a little more about who their child is spending their time with and whether they're going to be a good influence or not.

But why does the status of your boyfriend's parents' marriage come into it? Should it even matter?

I'm going to step back for a moment and try to see it from a typical South Asian parent's perspective. Just for a minute. Bear with me.

I can understand that, in some cases, a child coming from a single-parent household could mean they have dealt with difficult issues at home. Perhaps they suffered neglect, or trauma, or – at the very least – drama.

This kind of turmoil at home could have made it difficult for the child to focus on their education. Perhaps they had to go back and forth between two houses, making it harder to establish a routine. Perhaps they fell into friendship groups who had a bad influence. Perhaps they became distracted by other vices: smoking, or drinking, or something worse thanks to their home life being tumultuous. Or maybe the Aunties think they won't know how to commit because they haven't been around a committed and stable relationship.

After all, there's only one parent around who can keep an eye out, and there's only so much one parent can do.

Especially considering that parent could be struggling financially, as money may be stretched a bit thinner.

All in all, the situation culminates in what the Aunties fear: a lack of stability. And this, they say, is why children from single-parent families should be steered clear of.

There are, however, two problems with this way of thinking.

First of all, in my eyes, the things I've listed above are even more reason to give love and acceptance to someone who comes from a single-parent family. These supposed negatives aren't remotely good reasons for our society and culture to exclude people. We shouldn't cast out those seeking more stability in their lives – we should understand that they, more than anyone, deserve to find a safe, welcoming place to call home.

And secondly, it's insensitive stereotyping to assume a single-parent household always means a lack of stability.

Sometimes, the happiest children come from a single-parent family, because that single parent loved and adored their children like nothing else.

The irony is, most couples I know from generations before me probably should have done what's best for their children and themselves and got a divorce. Instead, they stubbornly stay together, forcing their children to be a part of their daily drama and domestics. They probably think they're doing right by their children, or maybe they don't want to face the shame and be labelled as a 'broken' family. But when you stay in a toxic environment, and especially when you're subjecting children to it, you're doing infinitely more harm than good.

The Aunties will never fail to mention it, eyebrows raised and tongues tutting, if someone is divorced and struggling. Yet, Auntie goes straight home from family events and spends a few furious hours arguing with Uncle, because he talked too enthusiastically to another Auntie, or he drank too much and caused embarrassment. Being married doesn't necessarily create happiness, and being a single parent doesn't necessarily cause unhappiness. Personally, I feel it takes far more courage to make the tough decision and leave a bad relationship or marriage, for the sake of yourself or your children.

Rather than turning our backs on young girls or boys who come from single-parent families, we need to wholeheartedly embrace them. We need to acknowledge that there's nothing for them to be ashamed of. We need to stop judging, and start understanding.

Being from a single-parent family does not make you broken. You deserve love and acceptance as much as anyone else.

'My parents keep trying to set me up on dates because they think it's time for me to get married now. I'm too scared to tell them I have a boyfriend.'

The time has come for you, my friend. You're at the 'right' age, according to your parents. The family will be making all the important decisions for you, from who the guy is to when the wedding will be. Eligible bachelors – please line up, and stay patient!

It's not just your parents that want to set you up. It's every single Auntie, and even the Uncles. I've found myself in many situations like this. Weddings can be the worst. You turn up to show face (and eat the delicious food) and, without a doubt, you'll be hearing the dreaded 'you're next' all day.

And at some point, you can guarantee there'll be a prying Auntie asking twenty-one questions. If it's not to set you up with her own son, then it's some other boy she knows. Or she doesn't know anyone quite right just yet, but she's more than willing to fill her spare time by starting a search party for potential suitors. She suddenly believes that she needs to lead the charge on finding who you should spend the rest of your life with. She probably doesn't even know you that well, yet this mission has become her number-one purpose in life. Hot Auntie's put you on the hot seat now.

Sometimes it's not even a question – they've just casually assumed that you're desperate for their assistance. *Hmm, I'll have a think for you*, they tell you thoughtfully and reassuringly. Um, okay, Auntie, all I did was tell you I'm single, that was *literally all*. And I only told you that in the hope it would end the conversation.

You could already be in a long-term relationship, and have found the person you want to marry. But you'll still tell family members you're single. Are we seriously going to tell a random Auntie who we barely recognise that,

'Yes, I do have a boyfriend, but no one knows about it. I'm enjoying dating without the pressure of someone asking when I'm going to settle down. I'm in love with him, but also I'm not planning to get married yet.'

I'm not sure she'll be the most understanding about this. Dating without the intention of getting the wedding date set soon? What does that *mean?!* (I'm also not convinced that your little secret would stay between the two of you. She'll have found a way to inform half the other Aunties at the wedding before the words have even finished coming out of your mouth.)

I've been asked a fair few times what my thoughts are on being introduced to a potential suitor, and I think there is a clear difference in being introduced, with the free option to say no if you're not feeling it, and a full-blown arranged marriage.

We've seen a lot of arranged marriages and how they work from the generations before us, and it really is potluck. Sometimes it works out, and sometimes it's beautiful. But every marriage comes with its challenges, and wouldn't you feel more motivated to make it work if you had freely chosen to be with this person?

I would also question, if the only reason to stay with this partner is to not let your family down after they made the choice for you, rather than out of any genuine affection on your part, how is it the right thing to do? How long can a marriage truly last if there's such a precarious foundation for why it exists?

As for simple introductions, I personally believe there is absolutely no harm. The only real risk is if it gets uncomfortable between you and the person you're being introduced to. It happens to us all: you say hello, and everything seems fine. But after two minutes you've completely run out of stuff to talk about and both quickly realise you never want to spend another excruciating moment with each other again.

After an encounter like that, there'll sadly always be a knock-on effect with your families. It could create a slight tension between the two families or some awkwardness during future meet-ups, and potentially the relationship between the parents fizzling out altogether. Any time my mum has suggested I meet one of her friends' nephews, or one of her nephews' friends, or so-and-so, the first thing I think about is how awkward it's going to be if the date goes terribly wrong and I strongly dislike him. But if everyone involved approaches it with the same attitude that it's just two people meeting each other, no pressure and no strings attached, as well as fully being prepared for it not to work out, then hopefully it can be kept light, only becoming more serious if both people want it to.

Even then, there's always a risk. Maybe you get on really well, you date for a while and possibly even get married. Eventually, though, maybe it doesn't work out. I'd be back at square one, worrying I was going to ruin my parents' relationship with their friend.

And if you meet someone totally independently, without the help of mutual friends or meddling parents, there's still the risk that it won't work out and you'll have your heart broken. Regardless of how you met, marriage is not easy. It's something to be worked at by both people, and there will always be challenges – no one gets to avoid them completely!

There's no such thing as love or commitment without risk. But that risk shouldn't put you off. If you get along with the person and sincerely see a future with them, then it's often worth it – as long as you feel it deep down. However you decide to meet people or start relationships, it should always be your choice rather than your parents' (or anyone else's, for that matter).

As for you keeping your boyfriend a secret while your parents are trying to set you up – this is tricky! Agreeing to meet the men your parents want you to could ruin what you have with your current boyfriend. At some point, you're going to have to come clean. There's only so long you can keep up the pretence.

If you're nowhere near ready to get married just yet, per-haps let your parents know that. To afford them some peace of mind, and so it's less likely they'll keep badgering you, you could give them a rough timeframe of when you think you may be interested. That way, they'll know that marriage is still something you can see yourself doing (if that's the case) – just not yet. Then, in the meantime, you can keep your boyfriend a secret until you think it's the right moment to tell your parents about him, without being pressured to meet other men.

And if you *are* ready for that next chapter of your life, then you need to think about whether your boyfriend is the man you want to live it with. If you know he's the one you want to marry, it should be easier to tell your parents about him – he'll make their search for your future husband a lot easier, after all.

Whatever you decide to do, I hope it's you who gets to decide your own future and fate.

Brown Girl Wisdom

It's so easy to get wrapped up in the pressures of society today. Our culture tells us we need to get married by a certain age and have children by a certain age. There's always emphasis on what we *should* do, rather than exploring what we *can* do or might *want* to do.

It's not just the brown community, either. As humans, we tend to aspire to an unrealistic idea of perfection. Then we punish ourselves if we don't achieve it.

We look at our phones and our computers, scrolling away through our feeds, and we watch other people showing off their seemingly perfect lives. Here's a girl who had a beautiful wedding to a handsome man when she was twenty-five; there's a guy who's expecting his third child at the age of thirty. We compare ourselves, without remembering that social media filters out all the bad bits. We measure our ideas of success against the polished perfection we see online. We analyse other people's digital timelines, and use that to determine the timelines for our entire lives.

This is something every single person in the world has to contend with, but I believe it's especially entrenched in the brown community. Look at Indian cinema, the world's largest film industry in terms of the number of movies produced, and therefore massively influential. Yet Bollywood movies paint an entirely idealistic, unrealistic image of what romance and marriage look like.

Should your entire life be based on the ideals society seems to have made up? If the people around you all seem to be getting married, does that mean you need to make it happen right now, too? If the people around you are having children, does that mean you should, too?

Well, think about it this way. If someone else jumps off a bridge, should you?

(Hint: no.)

The same principle should be applied to marriage, and having children: the fact that other people are doing it does not mean you should too. If you're going to make a big life decision, it has to feel right.

Most of us don't want to let the people around us down, particularly our parents. They raise us with love, and want nothing but the best for us, even if they don't always know how to show it. But if we only do things for their sakes, to satisfy them and make them happy, then how are we supposed to truly find our own version of happiness? How are we supposed to make something work and last when, deep down, our hearts aren't in it?

Sometimes, our families don't know what's best for us. And that's okay. They're only human, just like us. That's why it's so important to try to have open conversations – about who we are, what we want, and the boundaries of what we consider acceptable.

More and more brown girls are going against the grain, pushing boundaries, putting their careers first, or just taking the time to do what's right for them. Many more brown girls are getting married after thirty, or after forty, or deciding marriage isn't for them at all. Many are choosing not to have kids. Some partnerships, including those who are reproductively challenged or same-sex, may choose adoption or alternative ways of parenting. The same is true for parents who decide to stay single. Wouldn't it be totally insane, and cruel, to dismiss all of these people as being 'on the shelf'? There are so many different ways to have a joyful and fulfilling life. Being part of a heteronormative couple, with biological children all born before their parents hit thirty-five, shouldn't be seen as the default road to happiness any more.

You should marry who you want, when you want, and only *if* you want. It should be an option that you can leave for your entire life, or take when you feel it's right.

Marriage isn't easy. I've seen so many people around me, including my sisters, really struggle with it, especially during the first year. It isn't always how it appears in the movies. Most of the time, you haven't lived with this person before. And sometimes you're not just living with him, but with his whole family. It's a huge adjustment, and naturally it tests your relationship. It's so important to wait to take that next step until you know you can both face such challenges together and be prepared for what's to come. Then you can enjoy the great times, along with growing an understanding of how to deal with the hard times.

In the same breath, I say: it's your relationship, your rules. Your body, your rules. Your life, your rules!

To my ladies that are feeling the pressure to get married by a certain age, either because you've put this pressure on yourself, or it's coming from family members: I need you to know, it's never 'too late'. You won't be 'on the shelf'.

In anything I've ever done in my life, I've always felt behind others. Behind in my education, behind in my career, behind in getting married. But everything always seems to work out in the end.

I believe there is always a plan. It might not be your plan, but there is one for you. So enjoy the journey. You'll be even more pleasantly surprised when you find Mr Right, just when you least expected it.

Until then, live your life. If you've got your heart set on it, then don't worry – the big Indian wedding *will* come!

11

'YOU'LL HAVE A BOY NEXT TIME'

Boys continue the legacy.

Girls get lost to another family.

Boys will pay to look after their parents in their old age.

Girls are a financial burden.

Boys are a blessing.

Girls don't have value.

I was the third girl in a row, before my parents had my brother just a year after I was born. My eldest sister has told me that the difference in the atmosphere in the house when my brother came was worlds apart from my arrival. Looking back at baby photos and family videos, it's obvious that there was a lot more excitement and focus on my younger brother.

When I was born, my dad didn't speak to my mum for six weeks. Yeah, it was very dramatic. He didn't even hold me, or take any interest at all until my eldest sister, who was only eight years old at the time, noticed and pulled him up on it.

But when my brother was born, there were endless parties, congratulatory phone calls and family members hopping on flights from all over the world to come and visit. He was put on a pedestal from the day he was born.

My sisters and I were just what my parents had to get through to have him. That's how it felt, anyway.

Before having our little brother, my mum was under an obscene amount of pressure, for many years. She'd had a few miscarriages, which is a pain and grief I can't even imagine. Months before conceiving my brother, she'd read loads of books and spoken to doctors in India about the best way to have a boy. She changed her whole diet so that it was protein-heavy, which meant eating a lot of meat for most meals. Considering she's been vegetarian for most of her life, these were the extreme lengths she was willing to go to, just to have a son – and, by doing so, please my dad's side of the family.

With the age gap between me and my brother only being a year, growing up I could really see and feel the differences in how we were treated sometimes. One memory that especially stands out in my mind is from a time when I was around fifteen or sixteen. It was a Friday night. I had no plans with my friends after school and had decided to stay at home that evening. Meanwhile, my brother was off out, having a quiet night in at his friend's house.

'Having a quiet night in at his friend's house.' Hmm.

At around 1 or 2 a.m., I heard an awful lot of noise

coming from downstairs. I could hear my brother, but it didn't sound like he was alone. I walked into the living room to see around twelve or so of his friends. Guys *and* girls – usually in an Indian household you do *not* invite the opposite sex to your house, and most certainly not at that kind of hour, so my brother was already going above and beyond with breaking the rules. In addition, I could tell that everyone was extremely drunk, and could only assume they'd all come back from a house party. I walked into the kitchen and noticed my brother had set up his own mini pub, with my parents' drinks collection strewn across the breakfast bar. To this day, I have no idea how my parents weren't roused awake by the noise. But it was all going on while the rest of the family were upstairs, still sound asleep.

Straight away I thought, *Yes! Jackpot! He's no longer going to be the golden boy when my parents see* this!

I sure played my eager part in relaying the news to them straight away! I was not waiting until the morning; I needed them to see this with their own eyes. Yes, I know, snitches get stitches. But in this case, I was willing to do anything to show my parents that my brother *could*, in fact, do wrong, and that their perfect golden boy was no better or less human than me.

I was delighted to see him grounded and not allowed out to see his friends for a little while. But I couldn't help but stop and wonder: how different would the punishment have been if it were for me? I am certain it would have been way worse than just being confined to the house for a bit. That would have happened, but I would probably also have had my phone taken off me (this did happen on quite a few occasions), and of course got lumped with a pile of extra chores. Really, in comparison, how bad could it have been for my brother? Being grounded and not seeing your friends is pretty easy to get over if you get to sit around at home and play your favourite PlayStation games!

Now, I appreciate this story may seem a little childish, but it's hard not to notice the little things. Small moments can affect you. I've grown up constantly comparing myself to my brother, maybe in part because everyone else did. He's smart, he's kind, he doesn't really answer back and he definitely helps around the kitchen – what is not to love about him?

Unfortunately, it felt like I had to be all of those, and more, only to prove that I was anywhere near as good as him.

When we were much younger, my parents decided to move us from our local state to a private school up the road. I had to take an exam to get in and I remember feeling so under pressure to pass, not only because I knew my brother had already done so and been accepted (of course he had – younger than me and still always one step ahead), but also because I didn't want to be separated from him. Although I was going to be in the year above, I loved knowing I had him in the same school as me. I was also that overprotective type of big sister, the one that wouldn't let him fight any sort of battle on his own because I was ready to take on *anyone* for him. I knew he'd be fine without me, but maybe I wouldn't be fine without him!

Thankfully, I passed, and I was thrilled. Finally, I felt like I was on a par with my brother.

I was only in this new school for two years before it was

time to move on to secondary school. I applied for the same places as some of my peers (girls' schools only, of course), and I was a little worried about whether I'd be able to keep up with them academically.

To get into these schools, I had to pass yet another exam, so I spent months and months studying. Most of the preceding summer holiday was spent preparing for the exam. I really struggled to concentrate, but I put everything into it and tried my best. I ended up passing and it gave me a huge boost of confidence. No longer was I just trying to keep up with my brother – I was succeeding in getting into different schools, all by myself.

We were about to go and buy my new uniform and I was beyond excited.

Then, out of the blue, my dad told me I wouldn't be going. It would be a waste of money, he said. I was to go to the local state school that both my sisters had been to.

The following year, my brother applied for private schools too – going through the exact same process. He passed and we were all so proud.

And he actually got to go to that school.

He was worth the money, and I wasn't. I felt crushed, as though all my best efforts weren't enough. I wasn't worth it in a financial sense, which meant I felt I wasn't worth it in a deeper, emotional sense.

Looking back, I now understand that my dad, in his own way, was looking out for my best interests. He knew I would really struggle academically, and believed it might get too much for me. But at the same time, I wasn't even offered the chance to succeed. It was just taken away, without my say.

As a result, I didn't feel good enough, and unfortunately that feeling has stayed with me even into my late twenties.

Maybe because I'm a girl, my parents expected less. Maybe they thought girls aren't breadwinners or that they don't need a career. I can confidently say that, now, they don't feel that way at all, certainly not after seeing the professional successes achieved by their own daughters. I understand why they used to, though – they come from a time when men were the sole financial providers and the women stayed at home and looked after the children. The problem is that many brown parents still subscribe to this belief.

I fully respect if someone chooses to be a housewife – it is hard work. But what about the girls and women who don't want to be a homemaker? We should have the *choice*.

There are so, so many powerful South Asian women that I only know about now. The Vice-President of the USA right now, Kamala Harris, is a half-Black, half-Indian woman. From Malala Yousafzai, fearlessly fighting for girls' education, to Mindy Kaling, a queen of comedy and entertainment, we have so many incredible women to feel inspired by. I wish I'd been exposed to more shining examples like them growing up, rather than the only image of a successful brown woman being a Bollywood actress running around in fields, lip-syncing to songs and looking pretty.

Girls shouldn't just be expected to show up and look nice. We can all be so much more than that.

We're no longer obliged to take on work that fits outdated gender roles, and I'm not only talking about escaping the kitchen. Girls don't *have* to be models or club promoters, or any other job that's centred on our looks. Girls don't *have* to be receptionists or secretaries, or any other job that used to be defined by skirts and high heels. Girls don't *have* to strive to find a company that offers a good maternity package – legally, you can't be denied your rights as a mother or potential mother; plus, you may not want to be a mother at all.

All of these are jobs that men can do and be just as happy in and suited to. The boys should be encouraged to dress up and look glamorous, if that's what they feel like doing. Assistive and support roles are vital to any thriving business, and a man should feel just as proud in such a profession as a woman. And parenting is not a women-only affair, either; paternity leave is becoming just as crucial.

And on the other side of the coin, girls shouldn't be afraid to take on those roles that have been traditionally male-focused. Be the high-flying, sharp-suited banker if you like. Feel free to talk about or play sports without feeling intimidated. Get your hands dirty and become a mechanic if you like cars – being a woman doesn't mean you can only stand in the showroom and sell them.

Stereotypes about the work men and women are suited to need to be banished for ever. Women's skills and abilities are just as impressive, just as varied, just as worthy, as men's.

My sisters have daughters, and we now make a point of celebrating, loudly and proudly, every beautiful girl who comes into our lives. We never want them to feel inadequate or worthless, because we know they're anything but.

Of course, we still get those Hot Aunties hovering

around who say they hope it'll be a baby boy next time. They think we 'need' a boy now, after so many girls.

How do we deal with these Aunties?

Well, we tell them to stick it where the sun doesn't shine ... politely, of course.

Brown Girl Problems

'My mum gets me out of bed early on Sundays to help cook food, which is the one day I get to lie in after a long week at work. But she lets my bum of a brother sleep in till noon.'

Are you even any good at cooking? No offence – maybe you're amazing at it! But something tells me that it doesn't really matter.

For some reason, when it comes to doing chores, cooking and general household tasks, the expectation on boys is practically non-existent. It's always the girls being enlisted to peel the potatoes or hang up the laundry. Why, though? Being able to feed yourself or your family is an essential part of life, as is knowing how to maintain a clean house. These are not gender-specific roles; they are basic survival skills – we all need to know how to do this stuff.

I can imagine it's especially frustrating for you because you're already working hard in your job. Whereas your brother, I'm gathering, is not. I've known so many situations with a jobless, lazy, unambitious man who's just constantly given excuses by his mum to do nothing all day. 'The job market is very hard right now, of course he can't work!' 'He can't get work, so he's feeling down – of course he can't cook or clean!'

Whereas we women are expected to juggle it all. The worst myth I hear is that women are just *better* at handling more things to do than men. Well, I think men would be better at juggling if they were made to try it once in a while!

My advice to you is, next time you're told to get up and make food, make it really badly. Throw in too much salt, forget half the ingredients, accidentally put chicken in the chocolate pudding. Then they'll never want your food again!

I'm joking, of course. I'd recommend speaking to both your mum and your brother, and explaining how exhausted you are. You work hard and you deserve your lie in once a week. Your brother gets to rest a lot more than you do, so there's no reason he can't wake up early on Sundays and help!

Maybe, if they don't respond well, suggest you alternate weekends: you do a Sunday, then he does a Sunday. At the very least, he can't accuse you of being unfair.

Sadly, your brother probably knows he can get away with being lazy, especially if your mum is always giving him a free pass. So there's a chance they just won't listen when you try to make your case.

At that point, you have two choices: you can either stop trying, keep your head down and just resign yourself to accepting things the way they are. It's annoying and it's unjust, but it's a quieter life.

Your other option is to stand your ground. Lay out the boundaries. Be strict about what you're willing to do. It may cause some drama, some shouting and maybe even some tears, but if you don't budge, your mum and brother will eventually have to. And when the dust settles, you'll hopefully find that things have changed for the better.

'I'm one of four girls, and am so lucky to have supportive parents who never put up with spiteful, sexist comments from the Aunties. I wish other girls' parents could be like ours.'

Can we have a round of applause for your parents, please? In fact, a standing ovation!

Isn't it ridiculous that I have to make a big deal about parents who actually handle things in a positive way? It just shows how rare it is in our community.

I can't even begin to imagine the endless comments and questions your parents have had to face from all the Aunties, as well as those salty Uncles who don't see the value in girls. Apparently, carrying the family name forward is more important. Who even *are* you, Uncle? Royalty? I didn't think so.

In brown culture, we're too used to allowing other people to come right into our homes and our lives. We all know our Aunties and Uncles aren't even related to us half the time, yet they still merrily march right in and make their disapproving comments to our parents. A lot of the time, parents are happy to agree, or not say anything, simply to save face.

But their eagerness to save face just illustrates to their children whose side they're on.

It brings me a lot of comfort and happiness to know that there are encouraging stories out there, and families who don't care what gender their child is. Having your parents' unconditional support must help you to feel empowered, able to achieve anything.

People like your parents blaze a trail, allowing today's women and our future girls to know their value. Your parents' attitude enables young girls to know that it's okay to be outspoken, to disobey, to share unconventional thoughts and opinions. It doesn't mean you're a troublemaker, the black sheep, or any of the other dismissive labels pinned to girls who speak up.

No one is asking for parents to kick up arguments or fights. But it's clear your parents have the exact right approach. Simply brushing off the negativity, or not permitting someone else to speak badly about your family in the first place, can make all the difference.

The benefits of their actions don't just affect you and your sisters – they affect girls and women everywhere. It must be reassuring to know you've got such wonderful role models, should you ever become a mother to young girls yourself.

'My mum was told to abort me because I was the third girl, just like you.'

I can only imagine how tough it is dealing with pregnancy, in any context. Having to deal with it when people are telling you to abort the life you've created? It's just inconceivable to me.

If I think about your mum's situation in particular, she must have been reasonably far along in her pregnancy to know the gender – around twenty weeks. In the UK, abortion is legally only permitted in the first twenty-four weeks. How long were the Aunties trying to suggest she get an abortion for? I know I'm speculating, but it makes me worry. Were they going so far as to suggest she get an illegal procedure done? I really, really hope not, but tragically I still wouldn't be surprised. Sadly, for a lot of families, abortion is considered the only option when it's a girl.

What's worse is those Uncles and Aunties know what it's like to have children and create life. Auntie in particular knows what it feels like to get those flutters in her stomach, feel the kicks or movements, know that she is creating life inside of her body. It's unbelievable. To me, every child is a gift from God.

We come from cultures which are all about creation and vitality. So those Aunties will be at the temple one moment, praying to thank God for the sanctity of life, and in the next, they're spewing this negativity, trying to make a woman ignore that very same sanctity of life.

Now, I want to be clear – I'm not here to speak about my personal thoughts on abortion. I totally understand people's different circumstances, and firmly believe that every woman in this world should have autonomy over her own body. Choosing to have an abortion is something every woman has the right to do, if she so wishes. I can't, and will never, support forcing a woman to carry a baby to term against her will.

This is why I can't get my head around anyone trying to tell your mother what to do with her pregnancy. No woman should be forced out of an abortion; no woman should be forced into one, either. It's a huge decision, one that you should be able to make for yourself depending on what your beliefs are, and not because someone else is trying to influence you. Getting an abortion you didn't want could mentally scar you, permanently, and become something you deeply regret later in life.

No one, *no one*, has the right to put that on you.

It hurts to know that certain women, young or old, think they can have a say in other women's bodies. It's bad enough when the men do it. But the women – don't they understand the importance of having control over our own physicality? Don't they relate to the pain of having no access to period products, or getting backache because of a cheap bra that didn't fit? They should know, better than anyone, that each woman must have the agency to determine what happens to her own body. No one knows a woman, her body and her experiences better than that woman herself.

Each woman's personal history informs her own beliefs and decisions. My mum, for example, had quite a few miscarriages in between her children, hence some of the larger age gaps between us. It must be even more devastating to finally get pregnant, just for an Auntie to bring her bad vibes and tell you to abort the child you're pregnant with. How dare Auntie come barging in, acting like she knows best? She has no idea.

And all because the child is a girl.

Misogyny makes people callous. It means never imagining that a baby girl is just as wonderful, just as precious, as a baby boy. It means refusing to believe that women are just as much of a blessing to this earth as men are.

Misogyny means not valuing an innocent baby girl's potential. It means not valuing her life.

I feel as though I've spent my whole life trying to prove myself. I don't know if it's a consequence of knowing my arrival wasn't exactly celebrated, but I've always had a subconscious compulsion to prove to the world that I'm worthy. Especially after I took a more untraditional, creative path, the urge became even stronger. Not just because I'm doing something different, but because I'm a *girl* doing something different.

Knowing that some people in your community didn't even want you to be born, simply because you're a girl, must feel devasting. If I'm honest, I'm outraged on your behalf, as well as mine. We are both incredible women. Our lives are sacred, and should have been honoured from the start. We – like all girls – should be celebrated every day.

My advice to you is to think of your mum. She's clearly

another incredible woman, a real heroine, full of strength and love. She didn't succumb to the awful comments, because she knew your worth from the very beginning, as well as her own. She didn't let anyone else decide what would happen to her own body. She made her own decisions, and she put you before everything else. We should all try to be more like her.

If you're ever feeling down, remember what an inspiration your mum is: brave, independent and fierce in her love.

And you're a part of her flesh and blood.

Who cares what those horrible Aunties thought? You're the daughter of a goddess.

Brown Girl Wisdom

I know some of us brown girls have it easier than others.

In some households, the women and girls are treated horrifically. Rape, beatings, financial control, forced marriage, period poverty, female genital mutilation, maybe even going so far as honour killings or other murders. These are all appalling injustices and human rights abuses that would never befall any boy or man, and should never befall any person.

It's not just brown people, either – women and girls of all colours, all over the world, are suffering against odds which are stacked high against them. Even baby girls, who don't know that they're girls. Even those embryos who never got to be born and live as girls, purely because they *would* be girls.

I count myself extremely fortunate to have been born in

a loving family and environment where I'm not subject to such horrors.

But I know there are women in my life who have had to go through such things. I know there are Aunties in my life who have had to go through such things.

I'm very blessed to be happy and safe with my amazing family. To my sisters all over the world who are victims of worse sexism than me, I never want to pretend I know what it's like to be in your shoes. But I will still fight for you, because your fight is my fight too. I still experience the same sexism and lack of agency, even if in less extreme ways.

All of us brown girls, wherever we are, how big or small the injustices we're faced with are – we have one important thing in common: we're treated differently because of our bodies. Before we've even had the chance to learn, grow, develop a personality or show the world who we are, we're put into a box because of the bodies we're born in.

It does make me feel bad for our Aunties, when I step back and think about it all. That Mild Auntie, making a little comment about girls being too distracted by education these days? Maybe she never got to go to school at all. That Spicy Auntie, tutting about daughters who don't help out in the kitchen? She was probably tasked with cooking every meal for her family.

And that Hot Auntie, who seems so strict, so angry, so judgemental, about everything? Well, I don't know what she may have gone through to make her this way.

The way men treat us is a huge battle to be won. We should always be vocal against misogyny wherever we see it. If we are able to, we should donate to causes that protect women, raise awareness of what happens behind closed doors, and try to offer shelter and sanctuary to those women who have none. Let's do as much as we can for women everywhere.

Being realistic, though, it could take a very long time to overcome the sexism in our world. Men have dominated humankind for so many centuries, and societal change never happens overnight.

It's one step at a time, in my opinion. And men will never treat women better if *women* don't treat women better. We women need to band together. Urgently. The sexism we throw at each other only adds to the sexism we get from men and boys.

Next time an Auntie says something dismissive or biased about you, just because you're a girl, I want you to try something out – as long as you feel safe to do so, that is. As patiently and kindly as you can, ask her why she feels that way. See what she says.

I can guarantee that, at its core, it'll stem from experiences she had as a little girl.

This gives us the opportunity to start pushing back. We can start questioning. Where is the justice in this sexist way of thinking? Where is the compassion? Doesn't your Auntie remember how humiliating and frustrating it was, being stuck scrubbing pans while even her most lazy, disinterested brother got sent to school?

The burden to eradicate misogyny is not on women – it is on men. But those men will never listen if we're being complicit, mistreating our own, doubling down on the prejudices that the men already quite happily subject us to.

12

'YOU SHOULD STICK WITH YOUR OWN'

'Anchal, turn this off! Honestly, she's going to run away with a Black man one day if she keeps watching this kind of thing!'

This is one of the most prominent memories I have of my teenage years. My dad shouting at me for being too involved in Black culture.

I must have been around fourteen or fifteen, and MTV Base was playing some 'best R&B and hip-hop' playlist or another. Probably a lazy evening after school, or on the weekend, just sat there eating my food, vibing to the music in the background.

Clearly, this was unacceptable.

It was always about how listening to Black music, watching Black TV shows, or basically being involved in Black culture in any way at all, would suddenly end up in me 'running away with a Black man'. You have to wonder which bit was the bigger worry: me running away, or doing so *with a Black man.* Honestly, in some brown families, they'd probably prefer for their daughter to run away than to bring a Black man home.

As I grew older, in my twenties, those types of comments then turned into flat-out rules:

'You can't marry anyone Black.'

'You can't marry anyone Muslim.'

I guess I really, *really* can't marry a Black Muslim, then.

Seriously, though, no more sugar-coating – just straight out being told that entire races and religions are a complete no-no.

I questioned it. Loudly. Of course I did, because it made no sense to me. I would ask for reasons why. *Valid* reasons why.

And I would receive nothing back. Nothing. It was basically the classic shutdown, 'Because I said so.' And that was that.

I was confused, to say the least.

Like a lot of teenage girls in Britain, I had posters of various rappers all around my room. The best one was a totally *huge* picture of Lil Wayne above my bed. It made quite the impact. Then, one day, I came home from school to find that they'd all been removed. Just gone. No more Lil Wayne. As a kind of consolation prize, I was left with one or two of the smaller posters – stuck *inside* my wardrobe. For me to proudly look at whenever I was looking for an old cardigan, I suppose, but otherwise shut away. Kept hidden. Something to be ashamed of.

My parents are very house proud. They like our home to look like a showroom at all times, whether people are supposed to be coming over or not. If you're brown, you know there could be a whole host of random guests wandering about your house at any point, with no warning. We've had guests outright ask for a full house tour before, so many times. And my parents will go around showing them every nook and cranny.

I imagine I wasn't the only person who had to make sure her room was tidy if guests were coming over. It's as if your parents expect every guest to run upstairs and do a thorough room inspection (although, honestly, I think some of them would).

I get it. It's possible that my parents wanted my bedroom to be something resembling showroom standard. And maybe having gigantic posters of rappers with tattoos on their faces didn't quite fit that aesthetic.

Whatever their reason was, though, I didn't like it.

Just like the warnings over the music I was listening to, it was another way of sending me a clear message. Basically, to make me feel as though liking Black music, or being even vaguely interested in any figures from that culture, was something to be ashamed of. Like a dirty secret.

It's a painful thing to have to admit, but most of the time that's how it is when you're a brown girl with a boyfriend of a different race or religion. You have to keep them completely hidden; you have to ensure that you absolutely *do not* get seen with them.

I mean, let's be real, even if our boyfriend isn't of another race, we still have to keep him hidden! But that's more about waiting for the 'right time' to introduce them.

When's the right time to introduce a brown boy to the family? Pretty much as soon as the family thinks you're

the correct age to be getting married. Schedule the wedding, quick!

When's the right time to introduce a white boy to the family? He's still considered to be an outsider, after all. But if you've been together a long time and he seems like a dependable guy, then you'll get by just fine.

When's the right time to introduce a Black boy to the family?

Well, for some brown families, it doesn't matter if he's the most wonderful, loving, kind man in the world. It doesn't matter if he cherishes you and treats you amazingly. When it comes to picking the perfect time to bring him home, there *is* no right time. At all.

We already know brown communities suffer an intense battle with the problem of colourism. It's multiplied tenfold when we consider people who aren't brown. Yes, Auntie will make snarky remarks about a brown girl's dark skin – but she still considers that girl to be someone who belongs in her own culture, part of the community, one of our own. The biases against people who *aren't* brown reach different depths altogether. They become more vicious, more hypocritical – and, for the victims, more dehumanising.

We undeniably more readily accept white people into

our families than any other non-brown people. On my mum's side of the family we have a big fusion of cultures, and most of my cousins are mixed race – white and Indian. I've grown up used to this, and it's been subtly reinforced that it's acceptable and okay. When I may have shared a bad experience I've had from dating an Indian boy, I've received casual responses like, 'Try being with a white guy next time.'

Apparently, white guys treat you better. *All of them.*

I think what the Aunties and older generation sometimes fail to understand is that there's good and bad to be found everywhere in the world. A person's character isn't defined by their culture. Sure, I can try being with a white guy next time. He could be a philanthropist, or a successful business owner, or a witty and charismatic speaker. But he could also be a drunk, or violent, or someone with no life goals whatsoever.

For some reason, brown families like to gamble that the average white guy is going to have a positive impact rather than a negative one. All of a sudden, they actually want you to go On-the-Fence or Wild West. But if the guy is Black? Then who cares who he is, what he does or where he comes from – it's not even an option. Not up for discussion. You *will* remain By-the-Book. 'Because we said so.'

The only way it might be allowed is if you brought home the most stereotypical 'best of the best'. And what this really means is, you can bring home a Black guy – *if* he has money, and *if* he has influence, and *if* he comes from an established, stable background. He has to be exceptional, far more impressive than the fairly bland, unremarkable brown men that our Aunties married. Basically, if you're a brown girl bringing home a Black guy, he'd better be Will Smith or Idris Elba.

As much as I would love to bring either of them home, possibly even both, my chances of doing so are tragically slim.

Maybe one day, Will and Idris. One day.

But until that day, our brown families continue to judge others, simply by the colour of their skin, or the country their ancestors were born in.

I've been told a lot, by the Aunties and even my own parents, that 'it's better to stick with your own'. To some degree, I can understand where this comes from. Perhaps it just saves time and effort, having a partner of the same race as you – you don't have to explain and re-explain how you see the world and the experiences you've had, because they already get it. And there's an old-fashioned idea that raising a child is easier if both parents share the same culture. Perhaps there's less conflict and more consistency in the practices and traditions that child is encouraged to follow. If you're both By-the-Book, then you know you're reading the same book, after all.

I've tried 'being with my own', however, and I've not always had the best experiences.

My first ever relationship was abusive. I know now that he came from an environment where alcohol was prevalent. He himself didn't have a loving relationship with his own father, and had possibly witnessed abuse in his home. This kind of situation isn't uncommon, and the ensuing pattern can be quite typical – he grew up with a lack of love, and he brought a lack of love into our relationship.

How was I meant to have faith in 'my own', as I was instructed to? I didn't exactly have many positive male role models growing up, and then my first boyfriend turned out to be a toxic, hurtful presence. He was Indian. He was 'my own'. But after that relationship, all I knew was exactly what type of person I *didn't* want to be with.

As I've grown as a person, I've been affected by men who've hurt me and broken my heart. After experiencing so many moments of romantic disappointment, it's caused me to question the things around me a lot more.

Speaking with so many of my followers on social media, I've realised that they're also going through similar difficulties and confusion. They, too, feel uncertainty about stubbornly 'sticking with their own', since 'sticking with their own' has sometimes caused them real pain. It could be that they dated someone from a very traditional brown community, and realised that it isn't the life for them. Perhaps they didn't want to be the stereotypical daughter-in-law that their partner's parents expected. Perhaps they didn't want to deal with a man that was as judgmental as his family and had a say on all of your whereabouts. Perhaps it happened over and over.

Now, they're torn between facing the same problems yet again, or dating people of other cultures and backgrounds. Tentatively, they're starting to wonder about exploring the world outside of what they've always known. But after years of being warned of the dangers, that's not always an easy step to take. I think a lot of us brown girls have internalised this fear.

It's made me want to push back on these outdated, backwards, hypocritical views more.

Why do we act as though a man's character changes depending on whether they're Black, white or brown?

Why are we so rigid about learning and living with other cultures?

Why does everyone have a say in who we decide we want to be with?

I'm not accepting 'Because I said so' for an answer.

Brown Girl Problems

'I have a Black boyfriend and I'm scared I'll get disowned by my family. What should I do?'

The sheer fact that being disowned is not only a strong possibility, but pretty much a certainty, is what bothers me the most. We just know. It's something we grow up being so aware of. It's normal for us.

It's a threat that seems to roll off the tongues of our elders so easily. It's not just a scare tactic – although, even if it were, going this far to get your child to follow your rules should never be acceptable.

No, it's a genuine threat. You will be *disowned*. You will be forced to leave. Your family will disavow you.

How has being disowned become so normalised? It doesn't help that the Aunties – Mild, Spicy, Hot, all of them – absolutely thrive on the drama of it all. If a mother disowns her child, the Aunties vocally encourage that mother and get behind her, no matter what her motive was. Those very same Aunties will have no shame in calling round to see how the child is doing in the heat of the drama, trying to throw their two pence in where it isn't needed.

In conflicts like this, the Aunties will eventually pick a side. Either you, or your parents. Frankly, most of the time, it's going to be them and not you. Maybe, *maybe*, you'll get a particularly sympathetic Mild Auntie in your corner. But don't hold your breath.

I really wish that disownment wasn't such a relatively common way of handling things. It's so callous, and sharp. So final. What *does* need to be normalised is the Aunties sharing their embarrassment and condemnation for parents who reject their children. Because they're definitely sharing it with each other. 'How could they just cut all ties?' Spicy Auntie will hiss over her cup of tea. 'No sense of family at all.'

She has a point. Because a family has been torn apart – and over what? You falling in love with someone? Apparently, brown families believe that you being with the person you want, if they happen to be Black, is too shameful for them to bear. It seems that avoiding the embarrassment of it is worth losing their child over.

If I think about it, I wonder if our families' love for us is truly and deeply unconditional, if being disowned is even an option. It's not, is it? It's conditional – a 'do what I say', 'follow my rules', 'don't make me look bad in the community' kind of love.

I've had these thoughts and feelings before, and it can take you to an extremely difficult place mentally. It made me question how much my family could love me, if being disowned and cut off for ever is a possibility. But also, I questioned myself. How could I have so much trust in these people, the ones I love the most in the world – when at the same time, I know that if I took the wrong step, I could be ostracised and alienated from them for ever?

Who can I actually trust, if my own family could feasibly do this to me?

These were thoughts swimming around in my head for quite a long time, and they've still never fully gone away. Perhaps it's because I never approached my family about what I was going through mentally, and feeling that resentment while being unable to express it was enormously challenging.

I just dealt with things myself, quietly. But a part of me holds a grudge every time someone asks me why I'm not married yet, why I haven't found someone. All I can think about is the fact that I probably could have and would have by now, if I'd had the freedom to be with who I wanted to be with.

Instead, I've centred having my family in my life first. It's all I've done. So I've watched them be in relationships, get married, start families – all while I feel almost lost, torn and sometimes lonely.

The problem with being with someone not from the

same background as you, especially if they're Black, is that the possibility of being disowned is very, very high. And if that happens, will this man stand by you? Will your love be worth the loss of your family? You need to be sure.

If I'm honest, I hate this advice myself. It puts a lot of unfair pressure on you, to be certain about your relationship and future, and how can anyone be certain of the future? It can also put a lot of strain on your relationship, because you can't just enjoy each other's company and the bond you share. All of it's overshadowed by this creeping threat, and so you end up spending your precious time together desperately finding ways to make it work for the both of you, or for everyone else.

Unfortunately, things haven't progressed as much in this area as they should have, and our culture can still be incredibly backwards on this subject. If you're sure, really sure, that this man is who you want to be with, then disownment is, very unfortunately, the risk you have to take.

My advice to any parents out there: Yes, maybe some of the Aunties will judge you harshly, just because your daughter is with a Black guy. But disowning her won't change that. The Aunties will criticise you no matter what you do. A threat to disown may sometimes escalate into action, and then what? The relationship between your daughter and her Black boyfriend is still going strong; the Aunties are still tutting away; and you are now without your child. You'll still be the talk of the town, no matter what. You don't earn brownie points for cutting off your own kid; no one is going to pat you on the back for it.

I recommend that, instead of severing ties with your

child, you sever ties with those gossipers and stirrers who make harmful remarks. Then no one has to go through the pain of losing someone they love.

'I'm dating a Muslim guy, but his family want me to convert. How do I tell my parents?'

If your family is from a Hindu or Sikh background like mine, dating someone Muslim is sometimes seen as the equivalent of dating a Black person. And for many Muslim girls, it's just as forbidden to date or marry anyone outside of your religion.

Not to get too theoretical about it, but when you take a quick glance at India's past, a lot of the divide between Hindu and Muslim cultures is a sad product of colonialism. You can read heart-warming stories from Indians who lived in the early twentieth century and before; Muslims and Hindus forging deep friendships, working together, living together with respectful acceptance of each other's differences.

It wasn't all sunshine and rainbows, because history never is – of course there were conflicts, and wars, and injustices. But nowadays, the Hindu–Muslim divide is partly the product of the Partition in 1947. British India got split into two: India and Pakistan. It was a time of intense violence and danger, with people risking everything to get to the 'right' side of the border. It was, quite literally, a line drawn. A single community forced to become two.

Seems a bit of a shame, no?

Now, let me be clear. Someone's skin colour is not the same as someone's religion. Being a Hindu, Muslim or Sikh doesn't mean you're brown; being a Buddhist doesn't mean you're from Asia; being a Christian doesn't mean you're white; and so on. Where the colour of our skin and our ethnic background are unchangeable, our religion is something more personal. While there are sadly instances of people being forced to practise within a particular belief system, true religion shouldn't be about coercion – it should reflect a person's sincere beliefs and worldviews.

For these reasons, having differing religious views is completely separate to outright racism. I can understand why it would be incredibly difficult to try to build a life with someone if their beliefs don't resemble yours in the slightest. Because religion isn't just about rituals or books – for those who have faith, it's the very foundation of all they experience with respect to reality, morality and spirituality.

So yes, religion is important. There's a need for some kind of compatibility. If two people find they genuinely can't build a life together because of their opposing stances on fundamental issues, then that seems a fair and justifiable reason to part ways.

But if two people fall in love, and are accepting and understanding of one another's religions, why should this be so difficult to accept? Forcing these two people to stay apart feels a lot like drawing a line to tear apart a community – it's arbitrary, and unnecessary. It hurts so much more than it helps. The Partition all over again.

With regard to his family wanting you to convert – I can

understand why this idea may upset your parents. They've raised you, with love and faith, in everything their own lives stand for. They've done their best to educate you on your roots, your principles, and what being a good human means to them. No wonder you feel a little anxious to tell them that you're considering changing your belief system.

Although I believe all religions are essentially singing the same song, just with different lyrics, those songs may be heard differently to other people. Maybe it's to a beat they're unfamiliar with, or a genre they know nothing about and don't like the sound of. Yes, I know religion is nowhere near the same as a song or music – but even if it's in a light-hearted way, what I'm trying to say is that we don't all necessarily know everything about everything.

We may have heard an insult about someone else's religion or family, or we may have had a negative experience with a few people from a different religion. Does this mean we paint everyone of that faith with the same brush, and immediately judge and condemn them all to be the same? No. We may hear a rap, or a jazz piece or even a country ballad, and we may not like it very much at all. But then we find there are other songs in the same genre that we could listen to over and over again.

In other words, it's not fair to make judgements based on the few things we do know. We have to take each person for who they truly are, and base our opinion of them solely on our actual experiences with them. When we jump to conclusions about someone based on something like their religion, it's not just them we harm. It is ourselves too by depriving ourselves of the chance to explore a connection with someone who could have been exactly our kind of tune.

As for converting, it's a huge step. It is something you do with full commitment, not half-heartedly. If you're going to change your beliefs and take on the customs of another religion, then you have to be completely certain it's true to who you are. You can't fake faith. So, in my view, it's best not to convert if, in your heart of hearts, you're not prepared to fully immerse yourself in the religion.

Once you know you're doing it for yourself and not for anyone else, it might be a little easier to tell your parents. You're no longer telling them that you want to convert because of your boyfriend or boyfriend's family. You're converting because it's the religion you want to be a part of, and show your faith to.

No, this doesn't mean they'll accept it any more easily, but at least they'll know you made this decision for yourself, and not in order to be accepted by someone else.

'I've been with my boyfriend for four years, and now his parents won't let us get married because we're different castes.'

You'd think that, with all the fuss kicked up around other races and other religions, they'd at least let you marry someone of the same religion. *Surely?!*

But no. That'd be making it way too easy!

I won't generalise and say this rule goes for all South Asians, by any means, but caste systems are predominantly prevalent in Hindu and Sikh cultures. There's this pressure to get married, underpinned by the rules of who you can and can't marry on that all-important checklist I've mentioned before. 'Same caste' or 'better caste' are on that list.

For some families, the criteria for the perfect partner is almost entirely based around what caste they are. If you don't know what the caste system is, it's an ancient South Asian cultural structure which divided people based on their job and position in society, which still persists in many communities today. There's a definitive ranking of the castes, from the regal and respected to the lowly and shunned. And once you're in a caste, you stay in that caste – it's much more about your family name and history than what you actually do with your life. The only way you might move caste is through marriage. Typically, though, the people of the 'higher' castes want nothing to do with anyone from those 'below'.

It's basically an old-school hierarchy system, ranking people based on factors that have nothing whatsoever to do with who they are.

It makes even less sense for the families that moved to Western countries.

In my opinion, the caste system is outdated, prejudiced, and short-sighted. To put it politely, it's a load of rubbish.

Think about what it would mean in practice. Imagine going on a date, talking to someone, then asking, 'So what caste are you?' Urgh.

Sadly this has actually happened to me quite a few times when I've been on dating apps, or even in person. These are usually the By-the-Book brown boys – yep, they exist too. He might pop the question immediately over text, to know whether to bother continuing the connection. Or maybe he'll casually bring up his own caste on the date, so he then has the opportunity to casually ask you your own. Yeah, he's not as subtle as he thinks. *Taxi!*

I'm glad they ask, in all honesty. Please, feel free to reveal your real self to me at the start of whatever this is, because I'd rather find out sooner than later that you believe in this nonsense.

The world isn't how it used to be. We live in a modern, multicultural society. We now have the opportunity to travel to wherever we want and connect with whomever we want online. Sometimes you can't help who you fall in love with, and something as insignificant as their caste should not have any impact on whether you get married.

What do South Asian families gain from not allowing you to be together? Apparently, they favour their fake, man-made system which allows them to pretend that they're the pinnacle of society over allowing their own children to be happy.

I don't get it.

If you ask me, hang in there, sis. What you are going through can take persistence, but eventually something has to give. Either his family will change their minds, or the two of you will decide to continue your life together regardless.

It's not easy, but you'll know what the right thing to do

is when the time comes. I hope that it doesn't take losing his parents for the two of you to stay happily together, but if it does come to that, remember that it was their decision, not yours. You know you're coming from a place of love, not division. It's up to his parents to embrace that love, and if they choose not to, then it's themselves they'll hurt most of all.

If you know this person is for you and he's willing to hold on to you regardless of what his family say, then just hang in there. Love always wins.

'How do I deal with my Caucasian in-laws, who like to burst into an Indian accent and claim it's just a joke?'

Do we all start speaking the Queen's English and sound like we've come off the set of *The Crown* when we're around Caucasian people? No? I didn't think so.

So why is it okay to put on an Indian accent and act like it's funny?

It's not at all uncommon for South Asians to be victims of racism. It can happen at work, or on the street, or even at a friend's house. Sometimes it can be active aggression or mocking, other times we can be singled out as some kind of token representative for all brown people. Sometimes, we're ignored altogether. Simply for how we look, speak or dress.

There is a long-held conviction in many brown communities that white people are superior. It derives partly from our culture's deep prejudices with respect to caste and colourism, with paler-skinned people being regarded as society's richest and most influential. But there was also a big shift during the British Raj. India was ruled by the British as recently as 1947 – less than a hundred years ago. After decades of this colonialist hierarchy, I can understand why we still struggle to shake off the idea that white people are better than us. I can understand why we internalise the racism we experience, and subconsciously agree that we're the outliers, while whiteness gets to be the ideal status.

I like to remind my parents: no matter how much you favour white people, and believe that because you're not Black you're therefore closer to the same 'level' as white people – you're not. We're not. Even if you're the wildest Wild West brown girl there is, you're still a brown girl.

No one is ever, ever going to treat us like we're white. We are people of colour. We look different to them, eat other foods, dress in our own way, and sing along or dance to our own music. Yes, white people may happily embrace all of those things, but we will always be seen as different. If push comes to shove, we are always placed in the 'other' box.

I've downplayed my brownness in the past, just to fit in more. I've been so desperate for people not to have a reason to judge me – well, not one based purely on my skin tone, anyway.

I remember in an old job, I wanted to bring my own lunch to work. Hey, it gets expensive eating out every day, and I wasn't exactly rolling in the cash. Plus, my mum makes the most insane dishes – mostly Indian and always delicious. And as food is made in abundance in my house, there are always some leftovers for the next day.

So I took along my packed *rajma chawal*, which is basically a kidney bean curry and rice – so tasty. Lunchtime rolled around, and I went to the communal microwave to heat it up. Honestly, I was already feeling a little nervous, because I knew everyone in the staff room would be able to smell it. And, true to form, just as I walked in, one of my supervisors made a snide comment about how it smelt.

What you can smell there, my friend, is seasoning, flavour, the aromas of India – maybe you should try it sometime.

I know I'm making a joke of it, but at the time, I felt utterly humiliated. After that, I avoided bringing in my mum's delicious home-cooked Indian food. Someone doesn't have to be explicit with their racism, shouting derogatory terms or telling us to 'go back home' – these microaggressions can do just as much damage.

I feel people have been allowed to get away with far too much, for far too long. After all, it can be quite scary trying to fight the battle against it. Our grandparents and other elders have most likely had to deal with the worst of it, and probably wanted to live a simpler life without being racially abused and attacked, verbally or physically. So they kept their heads down. In ironically the most British way ever, they kept calm and carried on.

And I can understand why, and I respect it. But it does mean that British racism against South Asians is still a persisting problem in some circles. Maybe, inadvertently, we've allowed some of this racism to happen.

Times have changed. Instead of allowing these micro-aggressions to continue, we need to put a stop to them. I believe education is key. When confronting anyone who's being racist, you need to deliver a message, and you need to deliver it in the right way.

In your case it's your in-laws who are, whether they know it or not, participating in racist behaviour. People have no right to make fun of someone's accent. What may seem like a bit of entertainment to them can be immensely hurtful for the victims. Yes, there are sometimes words that we overemphasise, or articulate a bit differently. We pronounce them 'funny' because we've always heard them pronounced a certain way by our families. I do it all the time. I was born and raised in a Western country and don't have a hint of an Indian accent, but I still definitely say some words 'wrong', because I've only ever heard my parents or elders say them in their accent.

That doesn't mean I'm fair game to ridicule.

Perhaps your in-laws know exactly what they're doing and get a kick out of it, or perhaps it's just pure ignorance. Whatever it is, all you can do is simply explain why it is wrong, and why it hurts your feelings. Don't tell them they're terrible people, or that they're idiots. Just try your best to convey, in a calm and reasoned manner, that their 'joke' about Indian accents contributes to a false narrative, one where you're seen as weird, and lesser, and 'other'.

I don't know what your in-laws are like, though. Maybe they're not the kind of people you can approach in that way. You should always feel able to raise it with your husband, though. He loves you, and he can be your advocate. If you feel as though you can't speak to his parents directly, he can talk to them for you, behind closed doors. He can explain why these so-called jokes are not okay, and how much they've hurt you. After all, he knows them better than you do, so hopefully he can convey the message in a way that gets through to them.

I would hope you see some changes after that. But I would also keep in mind that people don't tend to transform overnight. If you do find it happening again, don't hesitate to remind them. By speaking up, whether it's directly or with your husband's support, you let them know that they won't get away with it again. Combatting racism can be a long and hard effort, but the result is so worth it.

Brown Girl Wisdom

There is so much in my culture that is beautiful and that I love. The flavoursome food, extravagant fashion, family values and traditions, as well as the best weddings ever ...

But there are some parts of my culture which, I've got to say, are really messed up.

As brown people in Britain, we experience racism first-hand. Yet some of us perpetrate this same prejudice against others – whether it's due to their race, their religion or their caste. We are victims of racism, so why don't we understand how hurtful our own biased attitudes towards others can be? Where is our compassion?

I wonder whether it's a result of defensiveness. Being a victim of racism is painful, and many of our elders suffered it when they first came to the West. It's so demoralising to be treated as something other than a human being, just because of your race, ethnicity or background. Perhaps some of our community feel the only way to regain control, and a sense of superiority, is by picking others to single out as inferior.

But it doesn't help anyone to repeat the same cycles of spite and ignorance.

Unfortunately, we're not where we need to be as an Asian community. There is still such a long way to go, especially with eradicating caste systems altogether, anti-Blackness within our cultures, and general unacceptance of others.

There is always going to be that Hot Auntie who wants to stir the pot, create more problems, and tell the world that you and your family are terrible people. But her accusations say so much more about her than they do about you. No matter how much we progress, she may never get over these prejudices. They're buried in too deep.

You have to remind yourself that it's her problem, not yours.

What's wonderful about life is that there are so many different types of people and cultures within it. It's stupid, in my view, never to learn to love and embrace others.

Stick to your own, if you really insist on it. But you'll miss out on all the incredible connections this beautiful world has to offer.

13

'MY LIFE WAS MUCH HARDER THAN YOURS'

You *never had to move to a new and scary country, to escape the violence or poverty of where you came from.* You *never had to start a business without a penny to your name.* You *never had to send money back home to family, while trying to take care of the family you have here.*

You *have food on the table and a warm place to sleep. You're lucky.*

So be happy, already.

Our elders seriously don't like to hear us brown girls expressing emotional pain or confusion. Summon up the courage to mention it, and it's highly likely you'll be shot down. Auntie will tell you all the harrowing tales of her own difficult childhood – how she only got to eat a couple of bowls of rice a day, how she never got to go to school, how she wasn't even sure she'd be allowed to stay in this country.

And she'll (loudly) wonder whether you'd have had the strength to cope in her shoes.

It's easy for us to trivialise our own pain or problems when we think about what our parents and grandparents, Aunties and Uncles had to go through. It's true that they battled against extreme odds to give us the lives we have. Like pretty much every other brown girl, I'm eternally grateful to them for everything they fought for.

But does that mean our own, different kinds of struggles count for nothing?

Everything this book has explored so far, from sex and dating to racism and appearance – it all has an effect on us. All the problems we face as brown girls. All the needling from certain Aunties and alienation from certain Westerners. All the sneaking around. All the cultural homelessness. All the unique pressures and conflicts that only come with being a brown girl.

All of our experiences build up, in our memories and in our hearts. Over time, it takes a toll.

Okay, Auntie, you're right. We may not have gone through the same physical, social and financial difficulties you did. And we appreciate everything you went through, with all our hearts.

But please try to understand: at some point in our lives, many of us have felt isolated, just because we're brown. Many of us have felt inferior, just because we're women. Many of us have felt so isolated and so inferior, so often, that it's developed into a full-on mental health condition.

What's that, Auntie? 'There's no such thing'? Ah, yes. Okay. Unfortunately, the majority of the South Asian community is woefully uneducated about matters of mental health. Conditions and experiences like depression, anxiety or addiction are not at all respected as real psychological ailments. Instead, it's generally considered that all people unfailingly have full control over their thoughts and actions. Any sadness or coping mechanisms are attributed, wholly, to weakness.

Imagine watching a TV programme with your extended brown family, where a character has depression. Let's say they cope by turning to alcohol and drugs. Listen carefully while you watch, and you might just hear your Mild Auntie give a little snort when there's a montage of the character going on a self-destructive bender. That little snort means: *Why would someone do this to themselves?*

Later in the show, when the character drinks themselves into a stupor, your Spicy Auntie will give a heavy sigh and an audible *tut-tut*. You can practically feel her contempt in the air. She's thinking, *They should just stop doing that.*

Your Hot Auntie agrees – of course she does. And she'll vocally offer up the final, damning opinion: *Such a shame that some people have these demons.*

Demons. Apparently, mental health maladies are the work of evil forces. And so the Aunties maintain that, if you're strong enough, you can fight those demons off. You need to just 'get on with it'.

If you're weak, however, you succumb. They believe it's all about your strength of mind. And your strength of mind is all about your blood. When it comes to welcoming a potential new son- or daughter-in-law, brown communities are fervent about researching entire ancestries. There's a fear that those 'demons', those 'weaknesses', are hereditary. They'll find some random, distant cousin who had a substance abuse problem, and they'll use it to dismiss the entire family as afflicted. They'll call it a shame, but they'll still decide the bloodline is irredeemable. *Tainted genes. Susceptible to demons and dark forces.*

These strong spiritual or religious beliefs are always very clear-cut. Like with most cultures, the prevailing moral code for South Asian communities stems from ancient texts and belief systems. Think of classic Indian epics like the *Ramayana* or *Mahabharata*. In each of these tales, the central focus is a climactic battle between two opposing forces. There's good, and there's evil; there's light, and there's dark; there's strength, and there's weakness. The binary is simple. There's never any room for a middle ground.

It's pretty obvious which side everyone aspires to be on. We all want to be the good guys, don't we?

I sometimes wonder whether parents believe they'll command more obedience and respect from their children by instilling fear in them of the negative, evil side.

Kindness, generosity and respecting your elders? Good and right.

Speaking out of turn or too loudly? Bad and wrong.

Modesty and humility in your appearance? Good and right.

The slightest hint of sexual promiscuity? Bad and wrong.

Being joyful and grateful for what you have? Good and right.

Feeling sad, uncertain, worried, lonely, lost? Well. Doesn't take a genius to work it out, does it?

This dichotomy is supposed to make us young brown people stay on the straight and narrow. But I worry that the exact opposite is true. We're not machines. That solid line between good and bad isn't the truth – it's all a lot more nuanced and complex in real life. We can rarely live up to the perfect, flawless heroes we're encouraged to be.

The result is, when we find ourselves feeling or behaving in a way that doesn't live up to that idealistic image of good-ness, we're terrified. It could be something as innocent as wanting to become an artist. It could be something as natural as same-sex attraction. It could be something as profoundly human as, sometimes, feeling upset or alone. Slip into any of these, or any such mild transgression, and we feel we're exposing ourselves as weak and immoral.

I believe this is the fundamental reason many of us brown girls and guys have to live so much of our lives in secret. And I think there's sometimes a very real risk of us being com-pletely driven away. For a lot of us, the choice is clear: escape your environment to get the support you deserve, or stick with your family to the detriment of your mental health.

I know I've been very fortunate never to have had to face that choice. You see, I've suffered with anxiety from a young age. For me, it always flares up in situations where I'm not in control of what's going on. For example, I remember occa-sions when I was a little girl, being at a family member's house for a morning ... and then an afternoon ... and then an evening ... and then into the night. Over the hours, as I steadily longed more and more to go home, the uneasy feeling in my belly would build. Finally, we'd get around to exchanging our goodbyes. As it kept going on and on, with yet more family members emerging or Auntie bringing along yet another Tupperware box of leftovers to take home, the feeling in my stomach would peak. I'd lash out and sulk and behave badly. I'd loudly announce that I wanted to go home because I felt sick – and it was true. But I'd always wonder why I felt fine, and full of energy again, the minute I was back home.

I experience this when I'm waiting in traffic, too. Or on long-haul flights. That feeling of waiting, and waiting, without any sense of control. Wanting to get to your destination but being stuck in limbo. It's got a psychological root, but it manifests both in your thoughts and in your body.

I always just assumed it was my own impatience, something I had to be stronger about dealing with and get on top of. But it was anxiety. I didn't even know it until I was in my twenties, but it was anxiety. It was nothing to do with me being weak.

I have had therapy in the past to cope with daily struggles, some of which were triggered by past trauma. When I began the sessions, part of me felt ashamed. After years of being immersed in a culture where mental health problems were dismissed as being caused by weakness or demons, I couldn't help but feel as though I'd failed a test. After all, my parents and my Aunties had struggled through so much in their youth, yet they'd never had the option of having therapy. What was wrong with me? Why did I need support when I had fewer hardships to battle than they did?

The therapy, as well as a lot of psychological self-care techniques and self-reflection, helped me to realise that there's nothing wrong with me. The experiences I've had in my life, both the joyful and the tragic, have shaped who I am. My mind is uniquely moulded by those experiences, and it reacts to certain things in certain ways.

I'm still on a journey, and have a long way to go. But therapy, and the understanding that came with it, helped me discover so much about who I am.

I know our parents and elders never had the option of therapy or psychological support. I accept that they truly did have to 'get on with it' in order to survive. But I wonder, is that such a straightforwardly good thing? Is their dogged determination against overwhelming odds an indication that they're stronger than us?

Or could something else be going on?

It's unquestionable that a lot of our elders had tougher lives than us, especially those who were first-generation immigrants, whether that be our parents or our grandparents. They also had access to very few, if any, sources of emotional support. Therapy was barely even acknowledged as a concept back in the day, especially not in South Asian communities.

The human brain is incredible. It's capable of suppressing the worst traumas, squashing the most difficult feelings, to help us survive. And so, it's entirely possible that our elders subconsciously had to bury their negative emotions in order to keep going and focus on the things they needed to.

Our mothers and fathers and Aunties and Uncles are human too. They're not immune to worries or woes. They're not resistant to loneliness and low spirits. Mental health conditions don't discriminate; anyone can suffer from addiction, psychosis or emotional instability. It's just that our elders never had the opportunity to get support for such feelings. So they had to act like those feelings weren't there. So much so, that they've even fooled themselves.

The sacrifices our families made for us went beyond the physical and financial. I believe they had to sacrifice so much emotionally, too. Because they continued fighting and kept going, they've given us a completely different environment to grow up and live in.

No, we no longer have to struggle like they did. No, we don't have to wonder whether we'll get to eat tonight or have a dry place to stay. But all of that safety and reassurance they gifted us with means we now have the freedom to be honest about our emotional struggles – a freedom they never had.

Mental health problems are nothing to do with demons, or weakness. They're a fundamental part of being human. The problem we have in brown communities is that there's shame attached to low feelings, but the truth is they're nothing to be ashamed of at all. In fact, the more ashamed of them we are, the worse they get.

It's time for us all to open up. *That* takes true strength.

Brown Girl Problems

'How do I tell my Indian mum that I'm start-ing therapy?'

First of all, let me say: good on you. I know the strength it requires to get yourself the help you deserve. You've had to have such courage to get yourself here. I hope the therapy is as life-changing for you as it was for me. After all, therapy helped me gain the confidence I needed even to write this book, and to finally speak up without feel-ing ashamed.

A few years back, I was in a bit of a bad place. It was actu-ally my eldest sister and my mum, watching me fall into a deeper hole day by day, who encouraged me to go and speak to someone. They'd both had therapy themselves, and they knew how valuable the experience is.

The person I was a little anxious to tell was my dad. I was worried he wouldn't understand. If I ever cried at home, my dad would always say, 'Why are you crying? You're strong.' Although they were intended as words of reassurance, my problems and feelings obviously didn't immediately go away as a result.

The scepticism and lack of education around mental health support in the brown community is a real problem. I can imagine part of you fears telling your mum about this important step because she may dismiss it as a waste of money or time. She may believe you just need to 'pull yourself together'. And she may tell you as such.

The idea of opening your heart up to your beloved mum, being so raw and vulnerable, only for your needs to be brushed off as unimportant ... well, it's enough to terrify anyone into staying silent for ever.

But staying silent for ever just isn't an option any more. Therapy is about openness, honesty and healing. Of course you want your mum to be aware. Her potential scorn about the validity of therapy doesn't really matter: she needs to know.

However, I have the feeling that that's not the only worry on your mind.

There's a chance your mum will be dismissive and defensive at first, yes. Just the same way she might react when she hears about someone else's mental health struggles. But she's your mother. You're her daughter. She isn't going to treat you like you're some faceless character on a TV show, or a friend of a friend of a friend she's heard about from the gossiping Aunties. Your story is going to be much more personal to her than that.

Your biggest fear, I imagine, is that you'll upset her. That she'll feel guilt. That she'll believe it's all her fault. Even if the reason you're going to therapy has absolutely nothing to do with her, somehow mums will find a way to blame themselves.

As a rule, Indian parents are thoroughly unacquainted with mental health issues. When they're faced with the reality of their existence, they can often be confused or overwhelmed. The cause-and-effect mindset that a mental health problem can be ascribed to a demon or to weakness also spills over into worries over their own responsibility. They did their research into family ancestry – you shouldn't be susceptible to any hereditary conditions. They taught you to be strong and independent – you shouldn't need to rely on therapy. Didn't they make all the correct moves, exactly to avoid a situation like this? This is where they start wondering whether they may have put a foot wrong.

Your mother has likely devoted much of herself to making sure you're content. Discovering that you're seeking psychological support may come across to her as a verdict: her one job was to keep you happy, and she failed. Knowing her child is in emotional pain will probably provoke intense guilt in her.

And that, in itself, will make *you* feel bad.

I don't know the circumstances that have led you to seek therapy. However, I'm going to say it's highly likely that you and your mum care about each other very much, and have never deliberately done anything to hurt one another.

Perhaps the environment your mother created as you grew up really did play a part in you starting therapy now. But that doesn't mean she ever deliberately did anything to make you unhappy. And equally, as tough as it may be to accept, her guilt is not your responsibility.

Therapy is a wonderful, healthy, positive thing. I truly believe that. Whatever the reason you're seeking it, it's something that can benefit pretty much anyone. Learning to understand yourself, learning to forgive yourself, learning to love yourself – they're all vital lessons, and therapy can play a huge part in your progress with each.

During my therapy, I felt proud telling people about what I was doing. I didn't feel ashamed. I likened it to going to the gym. We work on our bodies to maintain fitness, physically and mentally. It's the same way I felt about going to therapy, and opening up about the things on my mind. It's just another form of looking after your health – without the sweat and breathlessness.

My dad is right: I *am* strong. But strong girls need support too. Strong girls can have moments of so-called 'weakness'. And the strongest girls are those who learn how to make themselves feel stronger, if they want to.

I won't lie: I think telling your mum to begin with is always going to be difficult. I'm afraid there's no way around it. There may be shouting; there may be tears. There may be lots of questions. It's okay if you don't want to answer them just yet, as long as you communicate that to her, and let her know you'll share more when you're ready.

I believe you'll both get through it, and be so much stronger for it. Perhaps your relationship will change, but it will be for the better, because you'll be in a more truthful place with each other.

I do have some specific advice on how to tell her, though. Sometimes in conversations as emotionally charged as this, it's too easy to blurt things out and to express yourself incorrectly. You're both so tense, and not thinking things through. So my recommendation is to write her a letter.

I don't mean leaving her a note then running away in the night, obviously – I do still think you need to sit down together and have a personal chat. But the best way to break the news might be to put it all down on paper first. You can write it in whatever language you're most comfortable speaking to your mum in. You can have the time to really think it through, phrase things in a constructive, gentle way, and read it and reread it until you're sure it conveys what you want it to.

You might want to write about other brave brown people who have gone through mental health struggles. Write about Bhargavi Davar, a survivor of Indian mental asylums who went on to complete a PhD and become a leading academic in mental health discourse. And there's Reshma Valliappan, a diagnosed schizophrenic who's also an award-winning filmmaker and artist. You might even want to write about Shah Rukh Khan. Yes, every Auntie's beloved Bollywood hero once went through an experience of deep depression, which he's openly talked about in interviews, without shame. Not to mention one of Bollywood's most influential women, Deepika Padukone, for speaking up about suffering with depression, anxiety and panic attacks – things a lot of us go through.

Write about these successful, inspiring people, to show your mum that this is something that happens to many people, including people she admires and respects.

Then, when you're ready, you can ask your mum for some time to sit down together, just the two of you. You can give her the note, or you can read it aloud to her, or you can just use it to refer to as a basis for a freer conversation – whatever works for you. It's my hope that because you've put in the time to communicate with her clearly and compassionately, it'll make it a bit easier than trying to work out what to say as you go.

Best of luck with it, sis. It will be tough, but it'll be so worth it.

'I love my baby son more than anything, but since his birth, I feel like I can't bond with him and it's making me feel lower than I ever have before.'

In the brown community especially, becoming a mother (and especially to a son) is seen as the pinnacle of every woman's life – there is no higher achievement. Many Aunties and Uncles believe it's the single greatest thing we ladies can do. And, although it's not for the reasons they think, they're right in a way – whether it's to little girls or little boys, being a mother is a beautiful gift, and for many women it gives their life unique meaning.

That doesn't mean it's always rainbows and sunshine, however.

The NHS believes that postnatal depression affects one in every ten women within a year of giving birth. Ten per cent. That's a lot of women. So why don't we talk about it more?

I think there's a lot of stigma around postnatal depression because society – both Asian and Western, as well as beyond – only ever seems willing to talk about the joys of parenthood. In ads for baby food, we watch delighted mothers and babies rolling around in fits of laughter. In adverts for baby clothes, we see the adorable pastel shades, tiny bows and little animal designs. In ads for nappies, it's usually a montage of smiling, gurgling babies, who are portrayed as never crying, never throwing up, and never performing the very bodily functions that a nappy is required for!

I'm not saying we need to see every messy moment on TV. Certain things we know without needing to be explicitly shown them. But I *do* think that, as a society, we can afford to be much more honest and realistic when we talk about parenting. Because parenting is *hard*. Sleepless nights, anxiety when your baby is sick, trying everything to stop your little one crying but having no luck. Only a machine could go through all of that without feeling some distress.

Yes, being a mother is wonderful. It's also exhausting, and stressful, and isolating. All of those things can be true at once.

I'm not a parent yet, so I don't know what it's like firsthand. But I have two older sisters who are mothers. I've seen their struggles and, if I'm honest, the reality of motherhood I've witnessed through their experiences is completely different to the rosy image I had in my mind before. One of my sisters has suffered with postnatal depression, and it's not at all because she doesn't love or care for her baby. She does, more than anything. This same sister is a role model of mine, and one of the most inspiring, resilient women I know. I mean, she basically helped raise me. Both my sisters did. Seeing someone so 'strong' suffer with this condition was really challenging, and something we never expected – but it helped us realise that it truly can affect anyone.

Postnatal depression is non-discriminatory. But I believe it affects women in the brown community harder because there's such an idealised view of motherhood in our culture. A brown woman is supposed to feel nothing but unending happiness after they've had a son. So the shame and guilt that comes along with feeling depressed hits even harder.

Imagine trying to tell Auntie you're feeling down. She'd probably just say something like, 'Yes, I felt down for five minutes after I had my seventh son, but then I ate some mangoes and felt better.' Postnatal depression is barely acknowledged as a real thing, so rather than understanding that it's a known psychological condition, a brown woman instead feels she's just not a good mother.

Let me tell you: you are doing a *wonderful* job. Feeling low does not, in any way, cancel out your deep and everlasting love for your son. The fact that you haven't bonded with him doesn't undermine you as a parent. As I said, these experiences affect one in ten mothers who've recently given birth. That's a lot of women. You are not alone, you are not inferior, and you are certainly *not* a bad mother.

Postnatal depression is a serious condition, and it requires support. You deserve that support. Don't feel like your problem isn't important enough for medical help, because it truly is. It's rare that postnatal depression goes away by itself without leaving some long-lasting impact, but with the right medical help, the majority of women make a full recovery and go back to feeling like themselves again.

My advice, in the first instance, would be to reach out to your local GP or a health visitor. They're the experts; they've had the right training to help women just like you. Even if they can't directly offer assistance themselves, they'll know exactly who to refer you to for the specialist care you need.

You might also want to explore resources offered by organisations who support people with postnatal depression. There's PANDAS, who raise awareness and provide help for pregnancy-related mental health conditions, including postnatal depression. There's APNI, the Association for Post Natal Illness, who you can go to for telephone chats and online information. You may also want to check out community support groups, and speak to fellow women going through what you are – Netmums or BabyCentre are good places for this, and you can ask your GP about any local initiatives.

What you're going through is normal, but that doesn't make it okay for you to suffer in silence. Your feelings are totally valid. You do not need anyone to justify how you feel to yourself, or analyse or give you a list of reasons of why you're feeling the way you are; you just need someone to listen, understand and give you support.

Postnatal depression is an illness, and illnesses need treatment to get better. I hope you're able to access the care you have a right to, and make a full recovery.

Remember: your low feelings don't make you a bad mother. They make you human.

'I'm being put on some medication which is supposed to help me with my alcohol withdrawal, but my parents think it's just replacing one addiction with another.'

The fact you're going on medication means you've already reached out for help, and you're getting professional care.

I want to applaud you for that. Combatting an addiction takes so much strength, and it can't have been easy dealing with your parents' reactions as you secured your treatment. But you did it. You're clearly a courageous person, both for fighting against the urge to drink and for being open with your parents. You are *smashing it*.

You're now getting the professional care you should be, and are on a path to recovery. Sadly, though, it doesn't look like your parents feel the same way. They don't seem to understand the difference between self-medicating with alcohol and being prescribed a certified medication to help with the dependency.

In some brown cultures – definitely in my own, Punjabi background – alcohol isn't shunned. I've honestly had Punjabi guys on dates bragging about how much they can drink, even looking shocked when I say I myself, as a Punjabi, don't drink much. We often see Uncles lazing in their favourite armchair, whisky on the rocks in their hand, settling into their evening ritual. And as that routine becomes more and more normalised, an alcohol dependency can unfold right in front of us, and we don't even notice it.

On the other hand, many brown cultures fear any substance that has the capacity to alter the mind, even if it's only ever so slightly. We all know that one particularly Hot Auntie who won't even touch paracetamol. It's 'drugs'! And drugs are bad. All of them. Full stop.

It sounds like you've struggled with alcohol, so I don't need to tell you that some drugs genuinely can be bad. Alcohol is a depressant, and while it can serve to dampen feelings of anxiety or unhappiness for a while, long-term, it increases low feelings more and more. You've lived through all of that already, so you likely know it better than most people.

What I don't think our elders understand, though, is that alcohol dependency or other substance addictions don't manifest out of nowhere. I wonder whether brown parents realise that their 'get on with it' ethos pushes us young brown girls and guys into finding ways to self-medicate, rather than seeking professional help when we're down. An alcohol dependency often comes about because a person is in pain, but wants to keep it a secret. They're just doing what they can. But alcohol can't help with pain in the long term.

What our elders also don't understand is that certain medications and chemicals – ones fully sanctioned by medical and psychiatric doctors – actually *can* help.

It could sound a bit contradictory at first, I guess. But it truly isn't.

No, Auntie, you're not going to find any doctors recommending daily binges on alcohol or other recreational drugs. I don't even think it's an option on the prescription pad. But being prescribed medication by a doctor is a completely different thing. All right, it's still 'drugs' – but they're heavily experimented and tested drugs, with recommended volumes and times for use, fully endorsed by medical professionals as proven aids.

It's amazing how much our parents suddenly don't seem to trust doctors when medication is involved. You're always pushing us all to become doctors ourselves, Auntie – you can't pick and choose when you believe it's a worthy job!

Those trained medical professionals do, in fact, know what they're talking about. Yes, it's true that chemicals have the ability to alter our minds, moods and perceptions. But as long as your options have been explored and recommended by doctors, then that's not always a bad thing.

Fundamentally, whatever a doctor recommends, the choice is still yours. Medication, support groups, meditation, reading and research, self-care methods. As I'm sure your doctor has discussed with you, some or all of these options are available, and you need to choose the ones which are right for you. If you want to try the medication, that is not your parents' decision. It's yours. My hope is that your parents will see how much better you're doing on your prescribed treatment, compared to when you were self-medicating with alcohol. It may take some time, but they'll see it with their own eyes.

You've already fought the hardest part of the battle, my friend. You opened up, reached out and got yourself help. With bravery like that, I believe you can take on the world.

'How do you pull yourself out of a dark place?'

With all the adversity and problems we face as brown girls, we can sometimes get pushed to the edge. We're only human, after all. And day in, day out, we deal with quite a lot.

For some, it can get to the point where we feel we need to

self-harm for release. For some, it may even get to the point where we're considering suicide.

I'm not a doctor or a mental health professional, and I absolutely don't want to pretend like I can give you anything beyond my own personal experiences and opinions. But if you, sister, are feeling like you've reached the end, then there are a few things I want to say. From me to you.

You are loved. You are worthy. You are strong.

You don't deserve the pain you're going through. It's something that is happening *to* you; it's not who you are.

There is care and support and help out there for you.

You are still here. It can get better.

You are not alone.

There are many places you can go to for help if you're experiencing suicidal thoughts. I would strongly recommend you speak to your GP as soon as you possibly can. Please don't feel like what you're going through isn't important enough to raise, because it absolutely is. Your GP will be understanding, and they'll be grateful you made the decision to come to them. They'll point you to the right places for help, so you'll no longer have to fight the pain alone.

Before your situation even gets that far, there are ways to support yourself. You can download mental health apps that use mindful-based cognitive therapy to teach you how to overcome panic attacks and anxiety, as well as any other negative thoughts or feelings you may be having, no matter where you are. Some of these are:

- Be Mindful
- Beat Panic
- Calm Harm
- BlueIce
- Silver Cloud

For more immediate support, there are many services available for you to turn to, twenty-four hours a day. In the UK, you have the option of reaching out to Samaritans, who provide both a telephone helpline and email service for free emotional support. If you prefer to text, you can reach out to Shout, who offer free mental health help. There's also the National Suicide Prevention Alliance, who work tirelessly towards their goal of a world without suicide.

Samaritans
Phone: 116 123
Email: jo@samaritans.org

Shout
Text: 85258

National Suicide Prevention Alliance
Website: nspa.org.uk

If you're ever in immediate danger, please call the emergency services on 999. Your life is precious.

My heart and soul are with you. You deserve happiness, and I believe it will come to you very soon.

Brown Girl Wisdom

You are not alone.

We are not alone.

There are so many sources of help available now. In the UK there are organisations, like Samaritans, Shout, and Mind, solely dedicated to helping people with mental health problems. Approaching your GP is always a good idea, too. Remember your feelings are important, and worthy of attention.

I can say from personal experience that it's okay to get therapy – in fact, it's more than okay. Whether you're currently combatting so-called problems or not, it's a wonderful process which allows you to discover so much about yourself. The Aunties may roll their eyes or click their tongues, but ignore them. They haven't yet learned the importance of self-analysis and self-discovery. Honestly, I think they could benefit massively from a couple of therapy sessions themselves.

The brown community has not yet got to the point where they realise how crucial mental health support is. So if you're stuck in an environment where you're not allowed to express your emotional distress, it can feel completely isolating. But remember, there's a big community of brown girls out there, and so many of us fight the same battles. We know exactly the pain and the battles of our beloved sisters, because we've lived them ourselves. No matter how far away support seems, you are never alone. Your sisters from all over the world are with you.

There may be brown girls and other friends closer to

home, and it can be okay to turn to each other in times of distress. Keep in mind, though, that they're (probably) not therapists or doctors. They may be going through something themselves, so it's not fair for us to expect our friends to completely carry all our stresses and act as a constant sounding board. The point is that there are people in your life who cherish you, even if it doesn't always feel like it. People who appreciate your presence, and would miss you dearly if you were gone. People who want you to be happy.

I truly believe that our elders, despite their rigidity about traditional ideals and their doubts over matters of mental health, sincerely do want us to be happy. They just haven't realised the right way of going about it.

We need to teach the Aunties that prioritising your mental health does not mean you're resenting or rejecting your parents, culture and community. The old ideas of bad versus good, weak versus strong, simply don't match the world we're living in any more. We all know there are grey areas. We all know that what is good and right can't just be found by reading an ancient book. We're humans, and we're open to the vast range of emotions and experiences that entails. Sometimes, it's a joy. Sometimes, it's hard. And when it's hard, we need to be unashamed about reaching out for support.

We all need help sometimes. Admitting you need help is not a weakness. In fact, being honest about your own emotions and needs is arguably the biggest strength there is in life.

If you've learned how to reach out for help when you need it, then you're the hero of your story. It's as simple as that.

14

'FAMILY ALWAYS COMES FIRST'

Pretty much everyone has to face hardships in their lives. We brown girls have our own, very specific set of conflicts and obstacles we're forced to deal with. It can be distressing. It can be exhausting.

But being a brown girl comes with its benefits – lots of them. And one of the greatest benefits of all is our culture's focus on family.

We know that family is everything. We know it's the most important thing on earth. It shapes your beliefs, your ethics and your needs. My family has made me the person I am.

That's not to say it's always been easy, though.

In my family, we've been through so much. There were times my dad wasn't around, and some of the hurt from the fallout never entirely goes away. I'll always love him, but what we went through altered our relationship, because I've been affected in ways that can never be undone. I've discovered as much in my therapy sessions. I'm a happy, independent, bold woman, and I'm proud of who I am – but I'll always have particular fears and uncertainties as a result of what my family has been through. I always try my very best to forgive, but I can't forget. Sometimes, no amount of remorse or apologies can change the past. What's done is done.

This is why I believe it's so important to always put your family first, in actions as well as in words. Our families create us – in the worst situations, they can destroy us, too. I'm lucky my family has made it through, but we'll never be exactly as we were. The fracture that period caused can't be fixed. In some families, that fracture gets so bad that it leads to breaking apart altogether.

My experiences have taught me something vital. Family is about more than just blood – it's about who's there for you, who you can open up to, who you can be yourself with. I love my parents and my siblings; I also love my brothers-in-law and my sister-in-law, my beautiful nieces, my extended family, my Aunties and Uncles, cousins and second cousins – some of whom I don't share any blood with at all. They are my family, too. Sharing genes isn't the only criteria to make someone your family – far from it.

Your family are who you choose. It's your dearest friends, who hold you when you cry and celebrate your successes with you; it's your local community that has rallied around to support you during hard times; it's the people close to you, who you know will always be there, who you've let into your tightest inner circle. And yes, sometimes, it's even that gossiping Auntie you occasionally bump into at the post office and share a nice laugh with.

They're all your family. Brown families are big and sprawling, and not limited by blood or marriage – that's why our weddings always have a billion people on the guest list! If you've let someone into your heart, then they are your family.

And your family loves you.

The thing is, in brown culture, love often comes in unconventional ways. In many Asian families, most communication is done through rules and expectations. Maybe there'll be someone, like a parent or a friend or a sibling, who's a bit more tender and understanding – but, generally, all we hear is the rules, rules, rules. Do this. Don't do that. So-and-so is good. Such-and-such is bad. These are the lines, and you need to obey.

It can get frustrating, say, when your parents are badgering you into a career you don't want, or Auntie is coercing you to go on a date with yet another of her boring sons or nephews. It's true that this kind of pestering, when it really doesn't match our personal needs and wants, can make us feel anything but loved. Instead, we can feel ignored, or dictated to.

Although it can be tough to accept sometimes, this behaviour from our elders *is* love. It's just not conveyed in a way that *we* interpret as being love.

Why the disconnect? Well, I think of it like this: we're all speaking in different languages. Not vocal languages, necessarily, but emotional languages. We all have our own ways of communicating our emotional needs, and they don't always match. Perhaps the Wild West brown girl is speaking in a more Westernised dialect than the On-the-Fence brown girl. It seems like the By-the-Book brown girl does sometimes understand what the Aunties are saying, but not always. Our elders are speaking in the emotional language they know, that they were immersed in growing up, but it only makes sense to us brown girls some of the time. When we don't understand each other, we get angry, and we argue. Each of us begs the other side to just listen, and just understand.

Deep down, despite the mismatched modes of communication, I believe we're all saying the same thing. We're all expressing the same fundamental messages.

I love you. I want you to be happy.

Through our culture, we brown girls are lucky enough to be immersed in these messages more than most. And these messages, these feelings, are what it means to be a family.

If you ever doubt that brown families are typically bursting with love, just go and visit that especially Hot Auntie of yours for an afternoon. All right, she'll probably make some uncalled-for comment about your weight. And, okay, she may well complain that your Punjabi's gotten rusty because you speak too much English.

It's annoying. I know. And she *does* need to stop with the criticisms and unwanted opinions. We don't speak that emotional language, Auntie. It just makes us feel bad.

But, if you can, for a moment, try to step back. Ignore the insults. Observe what *else* she says and does.

The house will likely be even more spotless than normal,

because she respects your opinion and will have gone out of her way to make sure her home looks perfect for your visit. She'll constantly tell you to wear your scarf and gloves outside, because she remembers you had a very small cough the last time she saw you, and she wants to make sure you're feeling better. She'll have ditched the battered old Quality Street tin full of stale biscuits, and instead brought out a mouth-watering assortment of fresh snacks and desserts.

Speaking of food, she'll probably have made you an entire lunch. You assured her she didn't have to, but she wanted to. You need to eat, after all.

And if you're really too full to finish it, she'll make sure you take it home with you. She'll carefully ladle it into a plastic box and fasten the lid. Then she'll put an elastic band around the box. Then she'll wrap the box in newspaper. Then she'll put the package in a carrier bag. Then she'll stretch another elastic band around it.

Yeah, it's a bit excessive. But she just really wants to make sure the food doesn't spill in your bag. It'd be such a shame if you missed out on a single spoonful. Because as we know, for brown people, food *is* love. And even with her judgemental comments, Hot Auntie loves you.

Being a brown girl does come with its troubles. We all know that from experience. We're pulled across cultures; we have to deal with racism and sexism; we're often pressured to conform to an ideal that we don't naturally fit. It's hard, and I believe the Aunties and our other elders do need to work on improving their behaviour, so we can all live more harmoniously together.

But, you know, old dogs new tricks and all that.

I do think they'll learn. I have faith that those difficulties will get better for us brown girls and, in time, we'll all be speaking the same emotional language. But it *will* take time.

Until then, though, we're still very lucky. There are so many amazing things about being in a brown family, whether that's the family you were born into or one you found as you grew up.

A family's love is real, and eternal. They are your friends and your champions, your supporters through thick and thin. Whoever you have chosen as your family, be they biologically related to you or a 'chosen' family of close friends, you never, ever have to doubt that your family is there for you. They sincerely want what's best for you, even if they may need some education around what 'best' truly is. Your family has your back. Honestly, if they don't – if they genuinely believe that their social reputation is more important than your happiness, for example – then they're not your true family. Your true family is still waiting for you.

And no matter what, there's always our own family – our family of brown girls.

We live across the globe, in pretty much every country in the world. We're By-the-Book, and On-the-Fence, and Wild West, and everything in between. Some of us love to cook, while some of us are useless in the kitchen. Some of us play musical instruments. Some of us are engineers or doctors. Some of us love to laugh. Some of us love to dance. Some of us are gay, some of us are bi, some of us are straight. Some of us prefer not to date at all. Some of us were raised by single parents or adopted. Most of us have so many random Aunties and Uncles, we can't even count. We wear jeans, we wear saris, we wear beautifully embroidered tops that our mothers made for us. We eat *mattar paneer* and we eat McDonald's. We are all strong. We are all beautiful. We are all brown girls. We are a family.

Your brown girl family is out there, even if you've not met them yet. We sisters all understand each other, without even having to try. We know exactly what the Aunties are like, we know about *nazar* and the pressure to find a husband, we know those hours spent agonising over whether our skin is too dark or too blemished. We *know*.

We can cry with you when things have become hard. We can hold your hand, and give you hugs, and tell you how incredible you are. We can laugh with you when we see Mild Auntie attempting a sexy pout on Instagram, or hear Spicy Auntie sighing that Shah Rukh Khan hasn't divorced his wife to run away with her yet.

We are with you, even if we're not physically with you. No matter what's happening, your brown sisters are with you.

We are a family, now and for ever. And I believe we can get through anything, because we have each other.

15

'YOU'VE GROWN UP SO MUCH'

And here we are.

This book has taken us through all the ups and downs of brown girl life and, together, we've explored some of the things we often don't get to speak about.

We have a lot of Brown Girl Problems to go through in life – this book has only been able to scratch the surface. We face unique struggles in areas like romance, careers and appearance. We have to battle prejudices and cruelty, from both within the brown community and outside of it. What we have to go through simply cannot be fully understood by anyone who isn't a brown girl. It's our world, and our lives.

But these experiences make us strong, and they make us smart. We gain so much wisdom from the hardships we fight through. They help us learn more about ourselves, the things we want and the things we're capable of. Without the bad times, we wouldn't be anywhere near as appreciative of the good times.

And there are many, many good times. It's not all doom and gloom as a brown girl. Through our bizarre families and strange situations, we have loads of funny moments and stories to share. We get the hilarity of going on dates with guys who brag about their money, while their clothes show they *definitely* have no taste. We get to go to the best, most colourful and exhilarating weddings. We get to eat the most delicious food – in my case, lots of it.

With Bollywood, we get to watch the most insane films. Oh, a girl fell in love with a guy, but he died, but he didn't *really* die, and now they're on the run from gangsters, so they're singing a song with a hundred backup dancers who just emerged from behind the trees? Yep, okay, I'm on board.

We get to enjoy amazing fashion, culture and music, fusing both the Asian and Western worlds. We get a wider choice in the things we eat, wear and do. We get to explore what really fits.

We get to have each other. We get to share our weird and wonderful brown girl lives with our sisters.

And although it doesn't feel like it, we get to have the Aunties.

The Aunties may be strict, but they're also a real help to us. Their eagle eyes, their sharp tongues, their strict moral code – it's down to them that we brown girls are the well-rounded, quick-thinking women we are. Because of the Aunties poking their noses in, I've become a queen of hiding secret relationships, and making sure no one is barging into my business unless I want them to. Because of the Aunties being dismissive of creative and digital careers, I was more motivated than ever, and have become a successful online makeup artist and content creator. Because of the Aunties' blunt words and insensitivity at times, I've learned the importance of compassion, stepping back and trying to see another's point of view, even if they can't see your own.

After all, the Aunties were brown girls once, too.

I understand that they love us, and want what's best for us. I know everything they do is filtered through their own, often difficult, life experiences. But the Aunties can't define who we are, or decide our futures for us. They need to learn to love and respect us the way we are. And we need to accept them, too.

One day, we'll be the Aunties. The better our relationships with our own Aunties, the more we can use them to create better relationships with our own nieces and nephews. When the day comes that the young ones are giggling about our own spiciness levels, we want to make sure we're not dismissed as too Hot to handle. We want to ensure we're more sympathetic, more mindful of the things we say, and more accepting of the choices made by the people we love.

I can't thank you enough for coming on this journey with me by reading this book. It's my genuine hope that you've laughed, cried and cringed along with me and my experiences. I hope, more than anything, that this book has made you feel less alone. You have so many fellow brown girls out there, who've been through all the same things.

We've thought a lot about what the Aunties would say. Now, here's what I recommend we say back.

Parting Note to the Aunties

Dear Aunties – Mild, Spicy, Hot, and everything in between,

Thank you for sending me home with leftover biryani last week. I had it for lunch the following day. It was delicious.

I want to tell you some important things. I look up to you, Auntie. You're my family, and you mean a lot to me.

As a result, your words and actions affect me.

The way you rolled your eyes at my sparkly skirt hurt my feelings. It's my favourite skirt, I think it looks good on me, and wearing it makes me happy. That should be all that matters.

When you said that my boyfriend won't look after me properly, because he's Black, it made me furious. He's a kind, caring, lovely man, and I love him very much. His race has nothing to do with it. All that matters is how we feel about each other – and you have no say in that.

Auntie, I don't want your words and actions to make me upset or angry any more. For my part, I'll work on my own resilience and reactions. But for that to work, there are some things I need to let you know, too.

Here's what I need to tell you, Auntie.

From now on, I will no longer care about what you may say or think. If my opinions make no difference to your life, then yours do not make any difference to mine.

I am strong, I am independent, and I am able to make decisions by myself. I'm happy to be guided with your love and care, but, essentially, I make my own choices.

When I want your opinion – and believe me, sometimes,

I will – then I will ask for it. Giving advice that wasn't wanted just makes me feel as if you don't trust me. In turn, that makes me want to step away from you, rather than come to you more.

You need to understand that the world you grew up in is very different to the one we live in now. Being a little 'modern' doesn't hurt. Remember, you were probably pretty 'modern' yourself, back when you were young.

My mental health is important. I want you to think before you speak, so when you do, you're kinder and more gentle towards me.

Your mental health is just as important. I want you to be nice to yourself. When you look in the mirror, recognise that there's a beautiful, amazing woman looking back. You've been through a lot in your life, Auntie. You deserve self-care.

Basically: I love you, Auntie. Just … try to tone it down a little, okay?

Lots of love,

The Brown Girls – Wild West, On-the-Fence, By-the-Book, and everything in between.

RESOURCES

South Asian Therapists – A global directory of South Asian mental health professionals and therapists.
   Website: southasiantherapists.org

The Sharan Project – A UK-based charity providing support and advice to vulnerable women, particularly of South Asian origin, who have been or are at a real risk of being disowned due to abuse or persecution.
   Website: sharan.org.uk
   Phone: 0844 504 3231
   Email: info@sharan.org.uk

Samaritans – A free, confidential and 24-hour support service for anyone in need of someone to talk to, no matter how big or small the issue is, with zero judgement.
   Phone: 116 123
   Email: jo@samaritans.org

Shout – A free, confidential, 24/7 text messaging mental health support service for anyone who is struggling to cope.
   Text: 85258

National Suicide Prevention Alliance – An alliance of public, private and voluntary organisations in England who care about suicide prevention and are willing to take individual and collective action to reduce suicide and support those bereaved or affected by suicide.

Website: nspa.org.uk

Naz and Matt Foundation – A foundation that attempts to tackle homophobia triggered by religion to help parents accept their children, and provide support and empowerment to members of the LGBTQI+ community.

Website: nazandmattfoundation.org

Gaysian Organisation – Gaysians is the umbrella brand for the South Asian LGBTQI+ community. They bring together all resources, networks and organisations related to being queer South Asians.

Website: gaysian.org

ACKNOWLEDGEMENTS

I've always dreamed big, but I could never have imagined, even in my wildest dreams, that I'd be writing a book. This has been the most incredible journey, and I most certainly have a few people I need to thank.

Firstly, my management, Sophie Gildersleeve & Kim Riley. I remember during our first ever meeting together, I shared my podcast idea with you, and you instantly said, 'This could be a book!' I went home to my family and told them, and we all almost scoffed at the idea, but you believed in me and showed me that it's possible. You have worked endless amounts of hours with me to make this happen and put up with all my larger-than-life ideas. From the bottom of my heart, thank you.

I also have to say a huge thank you to Natalie Jerome, my book agent, as I like to call you. You have held my hand throughout this whole process and have been one of my biggest cheerleaders. It has been such an honour to work with you.

To my editor, Fritha Saunders, and the whole team at Simon & Schuster, it has been such a pleasure and an enjoyable time making this vision come to life. Swéta Rana, you have been an incredible support; thank you. I cannot forget to mention my talented illustrator Sookham Singh, who has brought life into my words through her artistic creations.

My family. You have put up with endless tears, mood swings, and excuses for why I can't clean the kitchen. It's all the little things you do to help me have more time to work on my dreams, and it doesn't go unnoticed. I'm genuinely grateful to have such hard-working and supportive parents. Because of you and all the hours you have put in, I understand how important it is to have a great work ethic and value small things in life.

I also couldn't be more grateful for my sisters who raised me and are my best friends, as well as a younger brother that I admire so much and have shared so many of my secrets with growing up. I can't forget the rest of 'The Sibs'; you are more than in-laws to me. I love you all so, so much.

I cannot forget my friends and my genie for keeping me going and growing with me over the years.

My followers; without you, none of this would be possible. You have been my inspiration and driving force for this book. If you have ever liked, shared, or commented on a video of mine over the years, I'm truly grateful. It's been a journey, and I'm deeply grateful to each and every single one of you. I'm sending huge air hugs!

Most importantly, God.

Thank you, thank you, thank you.

Thank you for everything you have given me in my life, and thank you for everything that is to come.